A Cooking Journey Through

COOKED
WEEKENDS
AWAY

Justin Bonello

PENGUIN BOOKS

Published by the Penguin Group
Penguin Books (South Africa) (Pty) Ltd, 24 Sturdee Avenue, Rosebank, Johannesburg 2196, South Africa
Penguin Group (USA) Inc, 375 Hudson Street, New York, New York 10014, USA
Penguin Group (Canada), 90 Eglinton Avenue East, Suite 700, Toronto, Ontario, Canada M4P 2Y3 (a division of Pearson Penguin Canada Inc)
Penguin Books Ltd, 80 Strand, London WC2R 0RL, England
Penguin Ireland, 25 St Stephen's Green, Dublin 2, Ireland (a division of Penguin Books Ltd)
Penguin Group (Australia), 250 Camberwell Road, Camberwell, Victoria 3124, Australia (a division of Pearson Australia Group Pty Ltd)
Penguin Books India Pvt Ltd, 11 Community Centre, Panchsheel Park, New Delhi – 110 017, India
Penguin Group (NZ), 67 Apollo Drive, Mairangi Bay, Auckland 1310, New Zealand (a division of Pearson New Zealand Ltd)

Penguin Books (South Africa) (Pty) Ltd, Registered Offices:
24 Sturdee Avenue, Rosebank, Johannesburg 2196, South Africa

www.penguinbooks.co.za

First published by Penguin Books (South Africa) (Pty) Ltd 2010
Copyright © Cooked in Africa Films 2010

ISBN 978 0 143 02669 3

Written by Justin Bonello and Martin Raubenheimer
Design and layout by twoshoes.co.za
Cover design by twoshoes.co.za
Cover image by Rodney Niesen Petzer
Photography by Duane Howard and Evan Haussmann
Printed and bound by 1010 Printing International Ltd, China

CONTENTS

FOREWORD

This book is a compilation of places, spaces, flavours and fascinations that I focused on while filming my cooking travel series 'Cooked', and it combines my three favourite things - Southern Africa, food and friends.

My personal gastronomic journey began when my late gran taught me to make pancakes *(I still have her pan many years down the line)* and during weekends and school holidays spent in the great outdoors either on the Breede River or on the Wild Coast in the Eastern Cape. This humble start was where I can truly say I began my love affair with cooking and wide-open spaces and my fascination with all the treasures of the sea.

By the time I reached my twenties I was getting it. The more you're out there playing, the more you understand the simple truths of food and life and how everything is interconnected.

And when you add into this mix the beauty of travel, of getting out there, of searching for those elements that make you tick, of making friends and memories, life is truly grand.

Today, I am still just a simple cook – I'm like any other South African, outside next to the braai, burning his fingers, cracking a can of lager and cooking for mates – but I hope that this book will inspire you to be a little more adventurous and to extend your repertoire.

Without exception, we all have flops from time to time - but, like life, food is about experimenting, trying new things, making good friends and, most of all, having fun. It's all part of the process and when it works the rewards are sweet - or savoury!

Just remember, those of you lucky enough to find yourselves in my marvellous part of the world have a duty not only to relish all that's on the menu but also to do so in a manner that's sustainable - I'd like my children to be able to experience my kind of life as well.

For those living farther afield and far from the veld - welcome to Southern Africa: it's a Moerse Lekker Place.

Justin Bonello
Cook, Traveller and Lover of Life

cooked // *translation* ① To have an unrestrained outlook on life. ② *informal* To be so infatuated with something that one seems fanatical, loopy or insane. **'That's cooked.'** ③ Off one's trolley. ④ To make food edible; Cooked to perfection.

Justin's colloquialisms & other translations

AFRICAN TV - campfire
BABBALAS - hung over
BEDONDERED - go crazy
BLATJANG - chutney
BLÊRRIE - excessively
BOEREKOS - local dishes made on farms
BOET - brother
BRAAI - barbecue
BUNDU - wild, sparsely populated region
CHIRP / TUNE - friendly banter
DERM - intestine
DOF - stupid
DOP - booze
DUK - fat
DUMPIE - small can of beer
EINA! EINA! EINA! - Ouch! Ouch! Ouch!
GAAN TE KERE - go wild
GESONDHEID - cheers
GOOI - throw
HOENDER - chicken
HOWZIT - short for 'how is it?'
ISIDUDU - crusty sediment
JOL - party
KAALVOET - barefoot
KRAAL - pen/paddock
KOP SEER - pounding headache produced by a hangover
KOS - food
KLAP - smack
KREEF - crayfish
KUIER - to visit and party on down
LEKKER - nice

MAAKIE SAAKIE - all good
MOER - bash
MOER KOFFIE - ground coffee
MOERSE DRONK - very drunk
MOERSE LEKKER - very nice
MUNG - bash
'N BOER MAAK 'N PLAN - a person will find a way
NOGAL - as well
NOW NOW / JUST NOW - any length of time from shortly to in a while
OKES - guys
OUMA - grandmother
OU TANNIES - old aunties
PADKOS - food one eats while travelling
PAP - soft porridge
POTJIE POT - three-legged cast iron pot
SCHLEP - big hassle
SKOP - kick
SLAGGED - slaughtered
SLAP GAT - very lazy
SLEG - useless
SPOEK AND DIESEL - brandy and coke
STUK - piece
TEN PAST THIRSTY - time to drink
TANNIE - aunt
VELD - bush/wilderness
VETKOEK - sweet/savoury balls of deep fried dough
VLEI/S - dam or marshy area
VLEIS - meat
WACK - load, big piece

When you've sneaked away a little early on a Friday, after the scramble of the week at work, it might be tempting, when you hit the country air, to sleep in the next morning. Don't do it. There's something magical about the quality of light when the sun first peeps out over the eastern horizon and spreads that golden glow across nature's amphitheatre. This is the best time of the day, so rise and shine. You're lucky enough to be far from the bright lights and out in the open and you have to break out and get cracking without delay. Heat up the coals and let the show begin. Have a hearty breakfast followed by a good strong mug of boeretroos and then seize the day with both hands and just kick back and enjoy.

Hitch a lift from Knysna. Catch a wave in Buffalo Bay. Sit on the sand and absorb an East Coast sunrise.

THE TIN CUP BREAKFAST

These are poached eggs - bundu style.

2 tin mugs
4 eggs

This basic breakfast allows for fillings of your choice - from mushrooms and crispy bacon to cherry tomatoes and mature cheddar and everything in between. Whatever combination gets you going! If it needs cooking (like bacon), make sure that you do that first.

Wipe the inside of the mugs with olive oil. Put in whatever ingredients you've chosen. Break two eggs over the top. Place the mugs in a pot with enough water so that the mugs are half submerged. Put the lid on and place it on the fire. Bring the water to the boil. This method of poaching eggs takes about four to five minutes, but keep checking. When the eggs are to your liking - eat them out of the mug with a spoon or fork. Ja, swaer, dis nou lekker.

ALWAYS TAKE YOUR ITALIAN CAMPING

Getting up at first light is what camping in the bush is all about. Sleeping bags and steamy breath, the smell of wood smoke in your hair and clothes and an enamel mug of good strong coffee in your hand.

Now there's only one way to make a decent stove top espresso on the flames and that's with a **Moka pot brewer.** All you need is a low to medium flame on your gas burner, a little water in the bottom, your special blend of finely ground coffee in the filter basket and in five minutes you'll be sitting pretty sipping proper moer koffie and taking in the sunrise. If you want to be a touch more eagle-eyed and are in need of a sun-upper, add a tot of brandy or a couple of slivers of freshly chopped chilli on top of the ground coffee before putting it on the heat - that's sure to open them blinkers and let the rays stream in! On the other hand, if you're after a mellower awakening, toss in a vanilla pod, a cinnamon stick or a couple of stuks of freshly chopped ginger and let the world unfold slowly before your eyes.

This was made on our way back from Mozambique. We'd spent five days travelling down from Bazaruto Island to the Wild Coast and we'd had enough of crab curry and other fishy comestibles. We were craving some solid boerekos and this was just the ticket. Think of a loaf of bread that's exploding with all the goodies you love in an omelette.

BREAKFAST BOMB

You'll Need 1 Well Oiled Flat-Bottomed ᴺᵒ·③ Potjie Pot

① First you have to make the dough. Put the yeast in a bowl, add the sugar and lukewarm water - if the water's too hot, it'll kill the yeast. Sprinkle some flour over the mixture and leave in a warm spot for about 10 minutes or until the yeast begins to froth. Then add the eggs to the mixture and give it a quick twirl. Next, make a well in the centre of the flour, add the salt and the yeast-and-egg mixture and knead until you have a smooth pliable dough. Cover with a damp cloth and leave in a cool spot while you get your filling together. *Take note that unlike most bread recipes, you don't want the bread to rise too much. This is because when you bake it, the bread will rise so high that it will squeeze your filling out of its case.*

② Working quickly now, fry each of the filling ingredients separately *(except the eggs, baby tomatoes and cheese)*. When they've all cooled down, crack the eggs into a bowl, whisk and add the rest of the ingredients including the cheese and tomatoes.

③ Roll out the dough into a big circle - think of a big pizza base - and place it in your well-oiled potjie pot so that the edges hang over the sides of the pot. Pour in your filling; this shouldn't be more than about 4 cm deep *(otherwise it takes ages to cook)* and then carefully fold over the bread dough and pinch the top closed. Put the lid on the potjie pot and bake on a fire by putting a couple of coals under the pot and a few on the lid. This needs to cook at medium heat. Too many coals will result in burnt bread, too few and you'll have undercooked egg.

As the coals die down, replace with hot ones. After about one hour open the pot - the bread dough should be crisp and brown. Stab the breakfast bomb with a skewer - if it comes out runny the egg hasn't set yet and the bomb needs to cook a little longer. If it comes out dry, it's ready to eat. Break off pieces and smear with chutney.

INGREDIENTS

for the bread dough
10 ml yeast
4 ml sugar
100 ml lukewarm water
2 free-range eggs
400 g flour
a pinch of salt
60 g butter

for the filling
6 eggs
1 punnet baby tomatoes
a handful of grated cheese
a handful of mushrooms
 - sliced
2 cloves of garlic
 - sliced and chopped
2 pork sausages
 - cooked and sliced
10 rashers of bacon
 - grilled on the coals
1 onion, medium size
 - sliced and fried
salt and pepper to taste
whatever else your heart
 can stand

Tip: Any left over dough can be made into fist-sized balls and cooked on a grid over medium coals for perfectly fresh rolls.

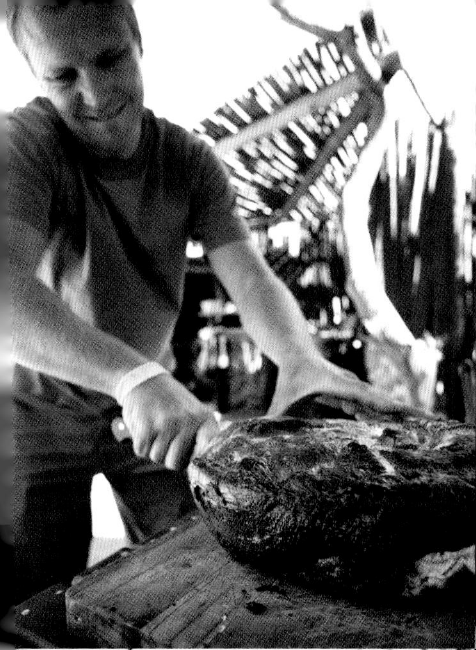
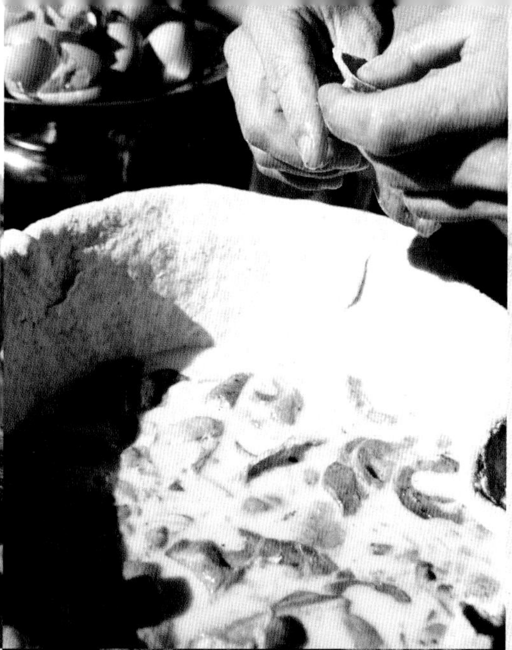
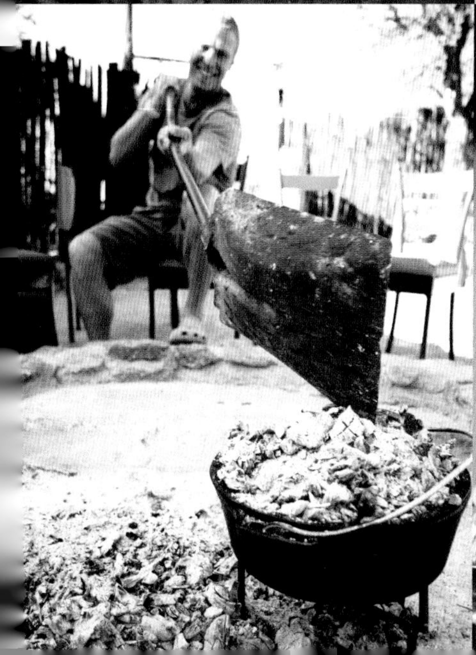
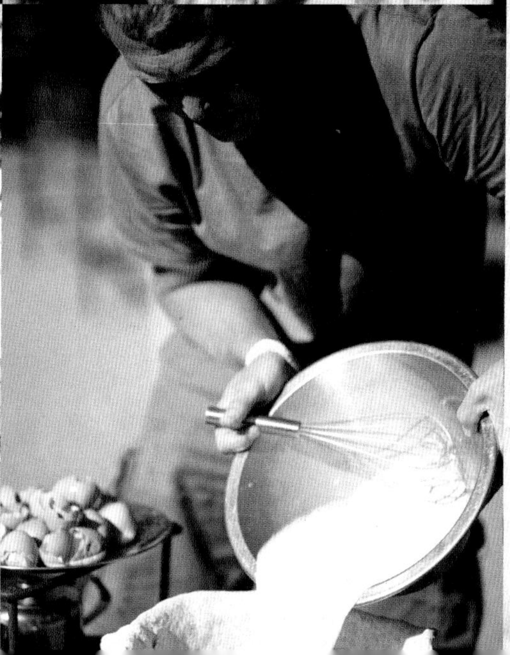

5.00

LESOTHO

086 6632 2815 0 0040
16 6632 2 15

202

0 0040

This is just a tad refined and is a really cool way to do a mass breakfast for your friends on your next getaway. It needs an oven - but even a gas one can cook these rippers.

BREAKFAST CUPS

Cut enough 10 cm x 10 cm squares of puff pastry to fill all the cups in the muffin tray. Line each cup with pastry and blind bake *(fancy term for partially bake)* in a fairly hot oven for about five to ten minutes - until they just start going brown. Then break an egg into each cup and bake until the egg just sets *(think soft-boiled)*. Now for the fun part - the toppings: if your tray has 12 cups make 4 of each variation.

① smoked salmon and cream cheese with chives or spring onions
② grilled bacon and mushroom with grated Gruyère cheese
③ tomato and mushroom with fried onions

Precook any ingredients that need to be well done *(like the bacon)*, then sprinkle, rip and tear the toppings over your soft baked eggs. Grill for three to four minutes. Serve hot with a twist of black pepper and a pinch of salt.

YOU'LL NEED

a 12 large-cup muffin tray
a roll of puff pastry
12 eggs

TOPPINGS

smoked salmon
cream cheese
chives or spring onions
bacon
sliced brown mushrooms
Gruyère cheese *(fondue cheese)*
sliced tomatoes
sliced onion

JAFFLES

Me Toastie Toastie Rise and Shine. Never leave home without a jaffle iron. Come to think of it, with electricity being what it is these days, don't stay home without one either. If you don't already have one, nick your mom's or look around second-hand shops. Then turn on the gas and go - you'll never look back.

This is the granddaddy of the snackwich and works on a gas stove, over coals or on an open fire. It's a really excellent way to use up leftovers and even not-so-fresh bread once heated through tastes like it's just come out of the oven.

If you don't have a clue what I'm talking about, let me explain . . . A jaffle iron looks like a long pair of tongs with identical convex circles of cast iron *(like earmuffs)* on each end. When pressed together these create a round pocket in which you place your jaffle.

• •

Butter two slices of bread and place one slice, buttered side down, into one pocket. Then fill with a generous helping of whatever filling you've got before putting the second slice on top, buttered side up. Bring the two halves of the iron together and close tight. Trim the corners of the bread if the iron hasn't chopped them off already. Place on the stove or fire and cook for roughly 2 minutes on each side. This isn't an exact science, so keep your eye on the prize. The outer shell of a perfectly cooked jaffle will be golden brown and crispy and the inside hot and juicy - any cheese in the filling must have melted. If you're watching the waistline, Spray 'n Cook can be used instead of butter but, as they say in the classics, everything tastes better with real butter.

Suggestions for fillings

tinned chilli con carne

crunchy peanut butter, sliced banana, and honey
(you can use jam instead of honey, but honey is the tits!)

ham, tomato, and cheese

curried mince

bacon, eggs, cheese and tomato - *a great breakfast in the bush*

just about any leftovers work well - *so mix and match*

This is a traditional recipe for bread made on a fire in the great outdoors or even in your own backyard. Doing it in the kitchen should not be an option but, okay, if you absolutely have to, then use the oven grill, but roosterkoek made on a fire just tastes so much better.

ROOSTERKOEK

First up, you have to activate the yeast. You do this by mixing the sugar, yeast and warm water together, then sprinkle a tablespoon of flour on top to prevent the mixture from getting a dry crust. Leave in a warm spot for 10 minutes or until frothy. Sieve the flour into a bowl, add the salt and then, using your fingertips, rub in the butter. Next, beat the eggs lightly with a fork and add to the yeast mixture. Make a hollow in the dough, pour in the yeast and egg mix and knead well until you have soft, pliable dough. Brush the dough with sunflower oil, place in big bowl, cover in cling wrap or a damp tea towel, and let it rise in a warm spot until it has doubled in size - about 40 minutes. Then knead the dough one last time.

Now comes the fun part. Break off a fist-sized ball of dough and flatten it with the palm of your hand. Put a good dollop of strawberry jam or chocolate or whatever you like in the centre and fold over. Press the edges down firmly and leave for about 15 minutes in a warm spot until it's risen to about double in size again. Then bake on a grid over medium heat coals until the roosterkoek is brown on both sides and cooked through.

If you're sitting round the campfire, wrap the dough around a stick and cook over the coals. When it's ready, remove the stick and fill the hole with strawberry jam and butter. You won't have to be told to lick your lips.

Moerse lekker with moer (ground) koffie.

INGREDIENTS

a pinch of sugar
10 ml dried yeast
100 ml lukewarm water
400 g flour
a pinch of salt
a knob of butter
2 eggs
sunflower oil

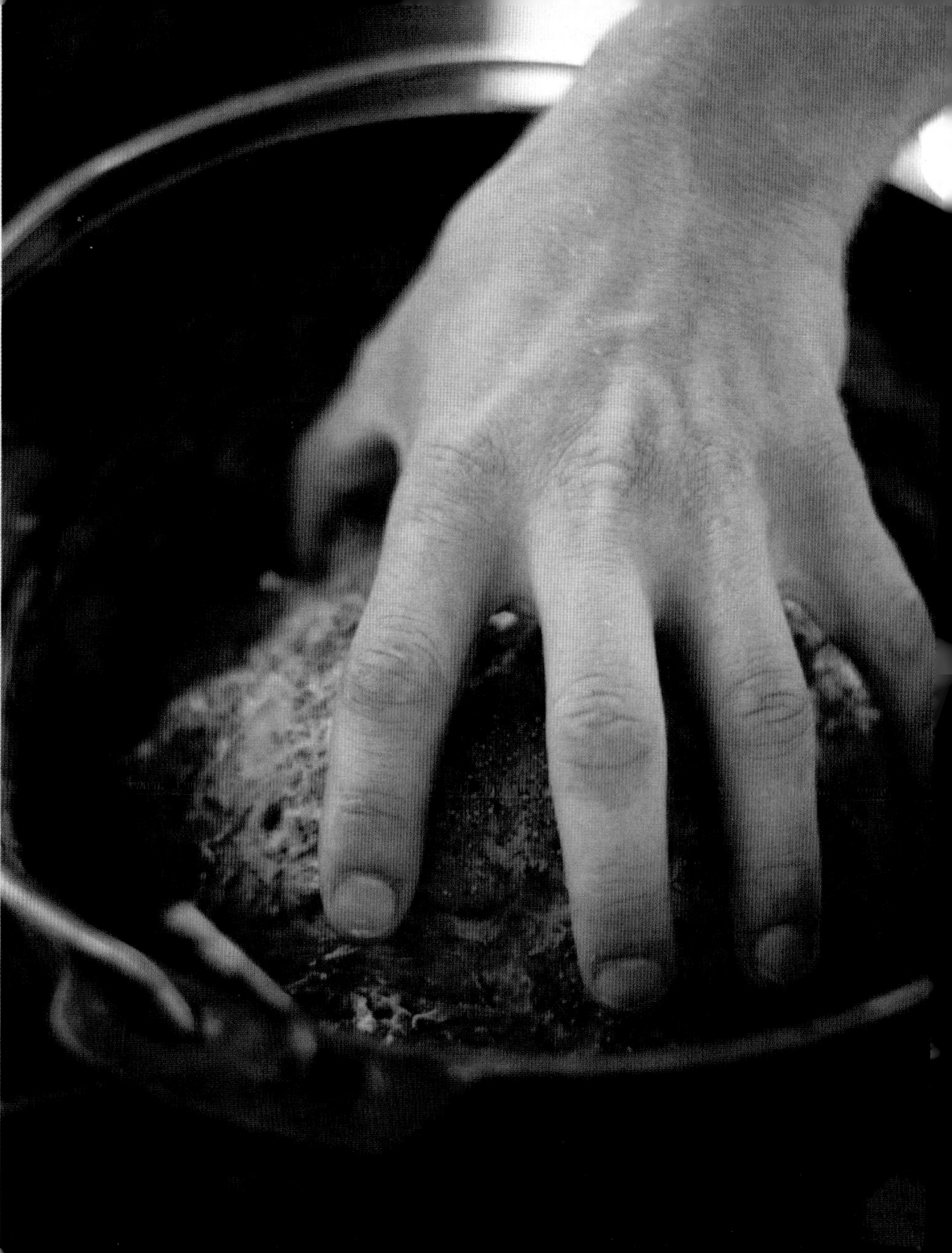

With fresh, crisp, steaming bread on the table you'll never go hungry. First thing, though, is to know how to make a basic bread dough.

POTJIE
BREAD

First activate the yeast. Mix the sugar, yeast and warm water together, then sprinkle a tablespoon of flour on top *(this prevents the yeast mixture from getting a dry crust)* and leave in a warm spot for 10 minutes or until frothy. Sieve the flour into a bowl, add the salt and then, using clean fingertips, rub in the butter.

Next, beat the eggs lightly with a fork and add to the yeast mixture. Make an indentation in the flour, pour in the yeast and egg mixture and knead it well until you have soft, pliable dough. Brush the dough with sunflower oil, place in big bowl, cover in cling wrap or a damp tea towel, and let it rise in a warm spot for about 40 minutes, or until it has doubled in size. Knead the dough one more time *(this step is called knocking it down)*, and then you're ready. Place the dough in a medium warm potjie pot, put the lid on and add a few embers on top of the lid to create an all-round oven effect. Bake for about 40 minutes.

BASIC BREAD DOUGH

10 ml dried yeast
4 ml sugar
100 ml lukewarm water
400 g flour
4 ml salt
60 g butter
2 eggs
sunflower oil

BEER BREAD

The great thing about this bread is that you don't need to knead it for hours and you can add anything from fresh herbs to sun-dried tomatoes or olives and fresh chillies to spice it up. This recipe makes one small dense loaf, or five medium-sized rolls, so adjust to fit the size of your pot and the number of friends for whom you're cooking.

Put the flour into a mixing bowl. Make a well in the centre, and pour about two-thirds of the cider into the well. Start mixing. Add just enough cider to ensure that the dough isn't too sticky or too dry - knock back what's left of the cider. Cover dough with cling wrap, put in a warm place and leave to rise for 20 minutes. The trick here is not to overwork the dough.

Shape the risen dough into a round wheel and place it inside the pot without rubbing with oil. Put the lid on and place a few embers on top of the lid. Remember to add fresh embers underneath the pot from time to time. The bread takes about 40 minutes to become crispy and brown and ready to devour.

INGREDIENTS

500 g self-rising flour
340 ml Savannah cider
   or a dumpie of Windhoek
5 ml salt
15 ml olive oil

5%alc/vol

SEAFOOD
02
AND EAT IT

By far South Africa's biggest neighbour is the ocean - our coastline stretches for more than 2 500km. This gives you a vast choice of locations, so get out there and spend some time on any one of our numerous beautiful beaches or if the fancy takes you nip over and visit subtropical Mozambique. And while you're out there trawling, be sure to try your hand at harvesting some of our treasures of the deep. Trust me, it's true that seafood caught with your own hands tastes just that little bit better. But be sure to purchase the necessary licence and only take out that which is permitted - our kids deserve to enjoy this privilege, and my uncanny bad luck, for themselves one day.

I've always thought of hoboes as gentlemen of the road, and since I have been doing all this travelling I have an even greater respect for them. When we finally reached Buffalo Bay I saw the look in the eyes of a gnarled old vagabond as he hooked himself a cob. I just knew he'd wrap it in yesterday's news and cook it on some driftwood while he sat on the sand and watched the light on the water at sunset. Who needs wealth or a mansion when you're flying high as a kite in such glorious surroundings?

HOBO FISH

INGREDIENTS

1 whole fish - *scaled and gutted* (*Kabeljou works really well*)

salt and pepper to taste

2 tomatoes - *sliced*

4 cloves of garlic - *crushed*

1 onion - *sliced*

This is like the fish in banana leaves (see page 34), except that you use wet sheets of newsprint instead.

Score the fish with a sharp knife, cutting slits about 5 mm deep and 4 cm apart in the skin on both sides. Rub with salt and pepper and stuff the belly with the tomatoes, garlic and onion. Wrap it in about 10 sheets of newspaper, wetting each layer well with seawater before adding the next layer.

Chuck the whole parcel directly on to the coals of *(preferably)* a wood fire and cover with more coals. Leave for 20-25 minutes, depending on the size of the fish. When you take the parcel out of the fire, remove all the charred newspaper and place it on a fresh sheet. Then eat it with your hands - hobo style.

I first tried this on the Transkei Wild Coast with a group of friends who were spending a lazy day on a mile-long white beach backed by cliffs and surrounded by rolling green hills. One of the mates caught a Kabeljou and literally moments later it was scaled, gutted and filleted and one half was baking on the fire in what was available - a banana leaf. If you can't get banana leaves, you can use tinfoil, but only as a last resort. Try your best to find some leaves - you'll go bananas for them.

FISH BAKED IN BANANA LEAVES

YOU'LL NEED

- **2 kg white fish fillet with skin left on** (Kabeljou, Steenbras, Cape Salmon or Elf, also known as Shad)
- **a handful of pitted black olives** - *squashed*
- **a very small handful of capers**
- **a couple of cloves of garlic**
- **a small tub of cream**
- **4 large banana leaves**
- **a few pieces of wire to hold everything together**
- **salt to taste**

Lay the fillet on a banana leaf and place a couple of olives, capers and crushed garlic cloves on top of it. Pour over about 125 ml of cream. Fold the banana leaf over and tuck the edges underneath. Continue to wrap the fish in the banana leaves until you have a sealed parcel. Secure the banana leaves with wire. Place directly on the coals, or use a grid if you have one. Let it cook for about 10-15 minutes, turning the parcel only once. Don't worry if the outer banana leaves burn and turn black because the inner leaves and the cream will prevent the fish from burning.

Serve with some bubbly and a green salad while sitting on the sand and staring out across the water at the horizon. Sheer magic!

Just a little suggestion: *Once you've made your stock or if you're on the beach and the gulls have finished picking, take the bones and guts and whatever else needs discarding, put it in a plastic bag and freeze it. You don't want this hanging around in the rubbish bin for too long because fish tends to go off very quickly. On the day the bin collectors come all you have to do is toss the bag in the bin, leaving your surroundings stench-free.*

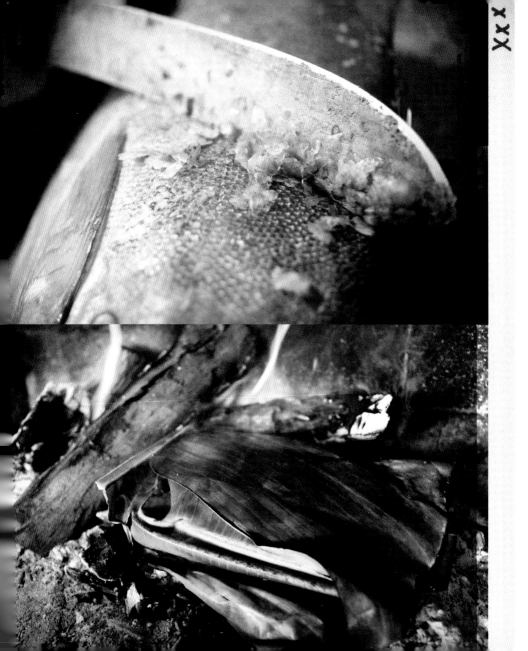

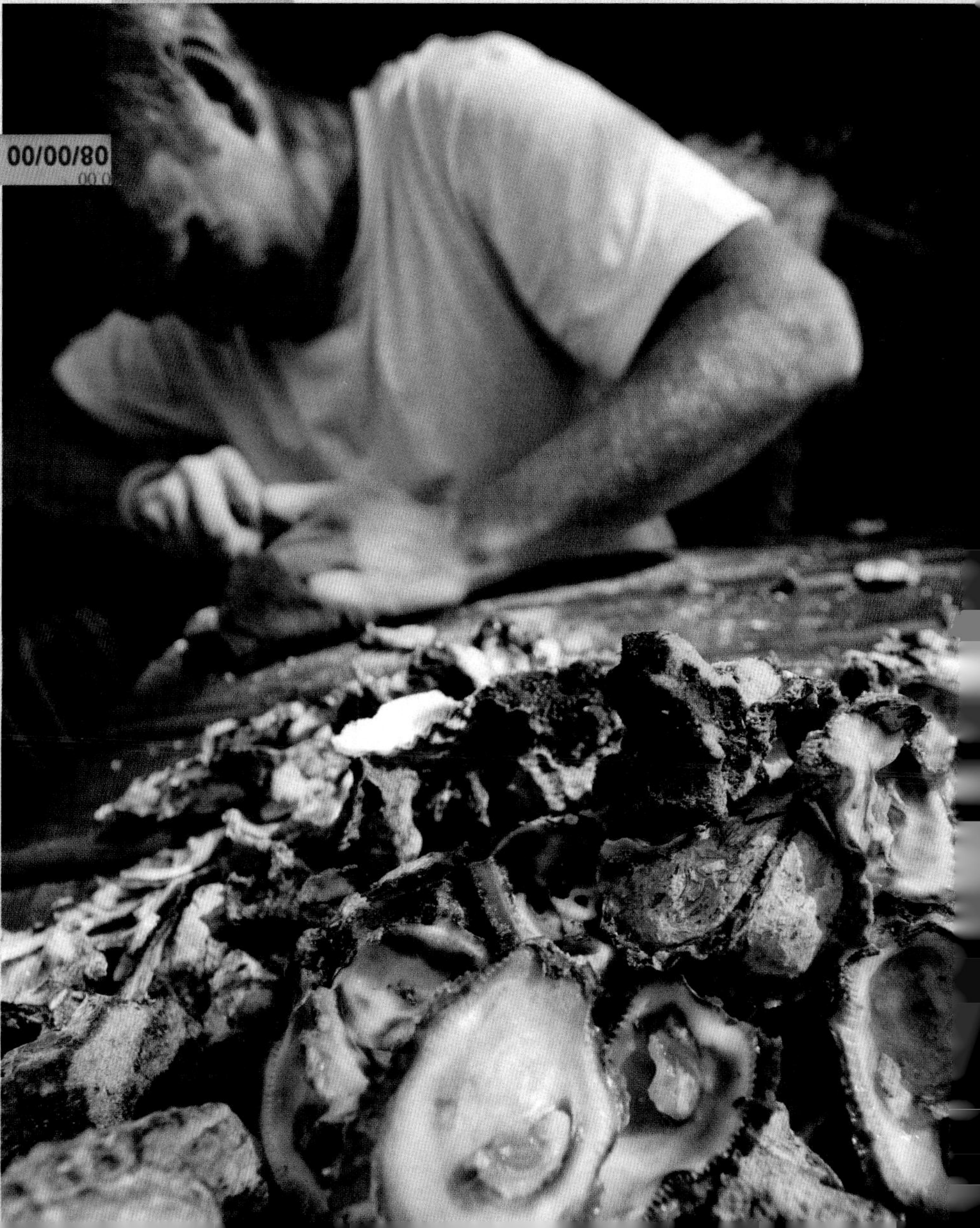

OYSTERS

Fresh oysters are so alive, so naked, and so much more pert than a bunch of wilting roses. So creamy, so fleshy, and so much nuttier than any box of chocolates. Shucking . . . drizzling . . . lifting and rotating to find the smoothest spot to kiss . . . and then to slurp. Gentle nibbles . . . the release of subtle flavours and . . . the clean, smoky aftertaste.

Serve with bubbly or crisp dry white wine, or maybe even a good single malt. Casanova and his many mistresses would devour fifty raw oysters while sharing a bathtub designed for two. Why not fill yours with sparkling wine?

But before you plan this wanton meal, there's a reality check.

SHUCKING

First up, you've got to find a supply of fresh oysters. Most good suppliers will open your oysters for a small additional fee, and it is worth every cent. But if you've found a spot where you can harvest your own, be prepared for pain. Live oysters can inflict serious wounds before they release their physical delights. So don't think that you can use a screwdriver or any old kitchen knife to open these babies. If you're really going to do this yourself, invest in an oyster knife, sit down outside and listen carefully . . .

Wrap the oyster in a kitchen towel, and place it on a flat surface with the small indentation *(the hinge)* facing away from you. Insert the oyster knife into the hinge and twist back and forth. Pry the lid open wide enough to hold it up with your thumb. Try not to plunge the knife into the oyster - the idea is to keep it plump and whole. Slide the knife along the top half of the shell. What you're trying to do is slice the muscle that connects the two halves of the shell and lift off the top half. A couple of small fragments of shell might break off, scrape these away, then slide the oyster knife underneath the body of the oyster and slice through the muscle that connects it to the bottom shell. Don't discard the oyster juice.

The first oyster opened is always for the guy who did it - slurp it au naturel. Now the bugger begins, you've got 2 dozen-odd to open, lad . . . but keep your eye on the prize.

From here on, things get pearlier. All the quantities given below are for 4 shucked oysters. Mix and match or serve them all. Unless otherwise mentioned, always eat the oyster with its natural juices.

Advice // Seafood poisoning sucks! So make sure your oysters smell of the sea and not of fish. If you press the top shell and it doesn't close, discard it. If you're buying them go to a reputable supplier like the Knysna Oyster Co. Maybe you should order in advance to avoid disappointment.

① Straight Up

A splash of Tabasco sauce, a little black pepper and squeeze of lemon juice. **SLURP.**

② Tempura Oysters

1 egg
**1 cup iced water or
  1 cup iced carbonated
  water**
1 cup all-purpose flour

Beat the egg in a bowl and add the water. Next, sieve the flour into the bowl and mix lightly. Be careful not to over-mix the batter. Dip oysters into the batter and deep fry immediately for about 20-30 seconds until the batter is golden and crispy. Serve hot with sweet chilli sauce.

③ Thai-style Oysters

In a small bowl, mix finely shredded ginger, chilli and sliced spring onions. Add a tablespoon of lime or lemon juice, a tablespoon of sesame oil and a tablespoon of brown sugar. Mix all these ingredients together really well and put a dollop on each oyster.

④ Garlic Poached Oysters

In a small pan poach the oysters for 2-3 minutes in garlic butter. Serve hot on wholewheat bread.

⑤ Angels on Horseback

4 rashers streaky bacon
  - *rind removed*
**freshly ground black
pepper**
**4 slices hot buttered
  brown bread toast**
**lemon wedges to
  garnish**

Remove the oysters from their shells. Wrap each oyster in bacon (*it's quite difficult, but worth the effort*). Season with freshly ground black pepper. Place under a preheated hot grill and grill for 3 minutes on each side or until the bacon is crispy. Serve on toast garnished with lemon wedges.

⑥ Oyster Shooters

tomato juice
Worcestershire sauce
Tabasco sauce
vodka - *a good dash*
celery salt
**freshly ground black
  pepper**
lemon juice

Make a Bloody Mary by combining the tomato juice with the rest of the ingredients. Place two oysters in each 'shot' glass. Pour over chilled Bloody Mary. Mix. Shoot. **SLURP.**

⑦ Sexy Lady

2 lemon wedges
6 slices smoked salmon
  - *cut into fine strips*
250ml crème fraiche
  (*sour cream*)
**a small bunch fresh
  chives** - *chopped for garnish*
red and black caviar
  - *go ahead, be decadent*

Remove the oysters from their shells, drizzle with lemon juice and wrap individually in a sliver of smoked salmon. Place a good dollop of sour cream on the end of each roll and garnish with chives and red and black caviar. Serve on a bed of crushed ice.

⑧ Divorce Cocktail

Lastly, if you've got no plans with someone special, try this one. Shuck an oyster, slip it into a shot of tequila, give it a squeeze of lemon juice, a drop of the hottest chilli sauce you have (*I use Mozambican Devil Sauce or Bushman's Dynamite*) and throw it back. Then wait to see if anything interesting happens.

BÃO

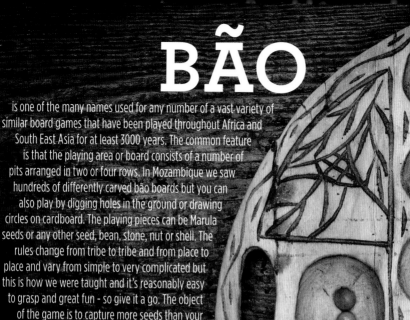

is one of the many names used for any number of a vast variety of similar board games that have been played throughout Africa and South East Asia for at least 3000 years. The common feature is that the playing area or board consists of a number of pits arranged in two or four rows. In Mozambique we saw hundreds of differently carved bão boards but you can also play by digging holes in the ground or drawing circles on cardboard. The playing pieces can be Marula seeds or any other seed, bean, stone, nut or shell. The rules change from tribe to tribe and from place to place and vary from simple to very complicated but this is how we were taught and it's reasonably easy to grasp and great fun - so give it a go. The object of the game is to capture more seeds than your opponent does. Our board consists of two rows of six pits. Each player owns the six pits closest to him. And two bigger pits called stores, which are used for holding each player's captured seeds. You need 48 seeds. At the start of the game these are evenly distributed in the 12 pits - four seeds to a pit.

Rules

START Toss a coin to see which player goes first. To make a move a player picks up all the seeds in any one of the pits in his row. Then moving anti-clockwise around the board, along his row to the opponent's and round again to his, he sows one seed at a time in each pit as he passes, until all the seeds in his hand are used up. If on any turn there are enough seeds in his hand so that he gets back to the pit at which he started then he must bypass that pit, leaving it empty, and continue sowing in the next pit until his hand is empty. Unless he is able to capture *(see below)* when his hand is empty his turn is finished and he 'sleeps'

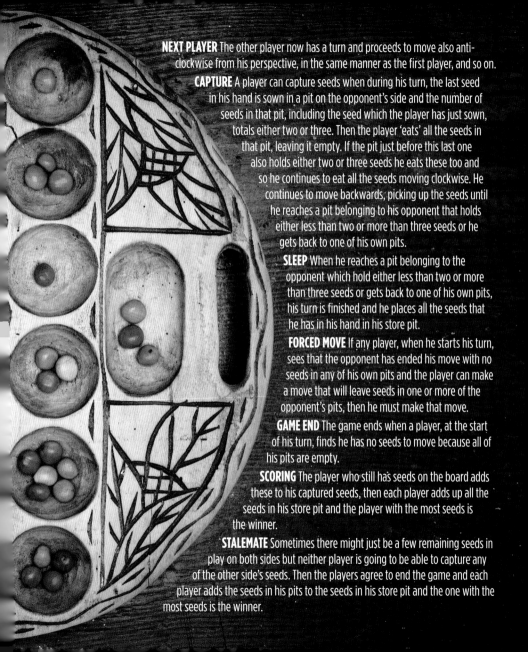

NEXT PLAYER The other player now has a turn and proceeds to move also anti-clockwise from his perspective, in the same manner as the first player, and so on.

CAPTURE A player can capture seeds when during his turn, the last seed in his hand is sown in a pit on the opponent's side and the number of seeds in that pit, including the seed which the player has just sown, totals either two or three. Then the player 'eats' all the seeds in that pit, leaving it empty. If the pit just before this last one also holds either two or three seeds he eats these too and so he continues to eat all the seeds moving clockwise. He continues to move backwards, picking up the seeds until he reaches a pit belonging to his opponent that holds either less than two or more than three seeds or he gets back to one of his own pits.

SLEEP When he reaches a pit belonging to the opponent which hold either less than two or more than three seeds or gets back to one of his own pits, his turn is finished and he places all the seeds that he has in his hand in his store pit.

FORCED MOVE If any player, when he starts his turn, sees that the opponent has ended his move with no seeds in any of his own pits and the player can make a move that will leave seeds in one or more of the opponent's pits, then he must make that move.

GAME END The game ends when a player, at the start of his turn, finds he has no seeds to move because all of his pits are empty.

SCORING The player who still has seeds on the board adds these to his captured seeds, then each player adds up all the seeds in his store pit and the player with the most seeds is the winner.

STALEMATE Sometimes there might just be a few remaining seeds in play on both sides but neither player is going to be able to capture any of the other side's seeds. Then the players agree to end the game and each player adds the seeds in his pits to the seeds in his store pit and the one with the most seeds is the winner.

About two hours up the west coast from Cape Town, and just around the corner from the little fishing village of Paternoster, you'll spot the lighthouse on the headland at Cape Columbine. The reserve owes its name to the barque Columbine, which was wrecked along this notorious coastline almost 180 years ago. The same cold and treacherous Benguela current that wreaks such havoc is kind enough to offer up the plumpest black mussels and Cape rock lobster - the bedrock for this delectable festive feast I'm about to share with you.

SEAFOOD PAELLA

✱ ✱ ✱ ✱ ✱   THIS RECIPE SERVES 6 TO 8   ✱ ✱ ✱ ✱ ✱

With a dish like this that has so many layers, timing is key. So if you decide to be a maverick and add or leave out a little here and there just be mindful that some ingredients take longer to cook than others. It's great if you have a two handled paellera pan but any shallow pan will do the trick - as long as it's big enough to take the quantity you want to make. If it's not, just use more than one.

① How To Clean Prawns / Rock Lobster
Pull off the head, then on the back of the prawn, slice open the tail and remove the dark thin line of the guts. This is called de-veining.

② How To Clean Mussels
Soak the mussels in a bucket of sea water, preferably overnight. This will allow them to spit out the sand and grit inside their shells. Next day, using a small sharp knife, scrape the mussels clean of all barnacles and other parasites living on the shell. Pull out the beard on the side where it pokes out *(the fibrous connections that attach the mussel to the rock)* and scrape this clean.

YOU'LL NEED TO GET YOUR HANDS ON

3 - 4 Cape rock lobsters

20 West Coast black mussels
- *cleaned, and de-bearded*

12 to 18 queen prawns

½ kg firm white fish
- *filleted and cubed (Kabeljou's good) and ask your fishmonger to give you the bones for stock*

300 g calamari cut into rings

FIRST UP   clean and devein the prawns and rock lobster, keeping their heads and half the shells for the stock. Roast them in the oven for about 10 minutes - this will really bring out their flavour. Marinate the prawns, along with the fish, in a mixture of brown sugar, lime juice, soya sauce, sesame oil, chopped garlic, ginger and chilli. Start making the stock by tossing the prawn and rock lobster heads and shells and fish bones into a pot with a little more water than is required for cooking the rice - this way you will allow for liquid loss while making the stock. Let the stock simmer, not boil.

Marinade for prawns and fish:

1 tablespoon brown sugar

juice of 1 lime

a splash of soya sauce

a good lashing of sesame oil

3 cloves of garlic - *chopped*

a hand of ginger
  - *peeled and chopped*

3 chillies
  - *chopped, seeds and all*

You'll also need:

a pinch of saffron

a handful of parsley

a glass of decent dry
  white wine

olive oil

2-3 cups of Basmati rice

4 cloves of garlic - *chopped*

2 onions - *roughly chopped*

2 hot chillies - *chopped*

6 ripe tomatoes - *quartered*

a few sprigs of rosemary

fish stock

a handful of mangetout

a handful of broad beans

1 red and 1 yellow pepper
  - *seeded and cut into strips*

2 punnets brown
  mushrooms

2 punnets hand crushed
  oyster mushrooms

6 chorizo sausages
  (or any other smoked sausage)

a lemon or two

NEXT toss the mussels and clams into a pot, add a pinch of saffron threads, break up the parsley and add, pour over a glass of wine and give the pot a good shake. Put the lid on and steam until the mussels open, as soon as this happens, remove from the heat. Discard any mussels that haven't opened, as they were probably dead when you picked them and could give you seafood poisoning. Retain the juice at the bottom of the pot - it's full of salty sea flavour and you can add some of this to the fish stock. But be sure to strain before use and add only a little at a time and then taste - it could easily get too savoury!

• •

To tenderise the calamari - moer it with any heavy object you have to hand; this is a sure-fire way of ensuring it stays soft and succulent. Splash olive oil into the pan and quickly fry the prawns and fish to seal. Remove and set aside. Be sure to cover them - remember flies are free and plentiful in Africa. Now fry the rice, the garlic, the onions and the chillies over a medium heat in 6 tablespoons of olive oil *(or as much as it takes to coat the rice thoroughly)*, stirring occasionally until the rice goes nice and translucent - the process is similar to Risotto. Then add the calamari, tomatoes, rosemary, and stock. Seal the dish with tin foil, and allow it to cook until the rice is almost done. You can do this either in an oven at 180°C, or on a fire at low heat.

• •

Remove the tinfoil *(keep it in one piece because you're going to use it again)* and drop the following into the rice: half of the mangetout, broad beans, peppers, both kinds of mushrooms, and all the fish, prawns and mussels. Seal again and put back on the heat until the rice is cooked. You're allowed to peek every now and then and taste as well - this is one of the perks of being the officer in charge. You may need to add more stock. Just before you dish up add the remainder of the vegetables - they'll give the paella a lovely fresh crunch - and the chorizo sausage. Season to taste, give it all a good toss and serve immediately with a squeeze of lemon juice.

• •

Important: Don't stir the rice while it's cooking - you'll destroy the channels that help the flavour of the stock to permeate the grains. Remember, too, to check the instructions on the packet with regard to rice vs liquid quantities. I use 1 cup rice to 1½ cups liquid, but it might differ from brand to brand.

Saffron is intrinsic to paella. It comes from southwest Asia and has been known for decades as the world's most expensive spice by weight. This is because it is hand harvested from the flower of the saffron crocus of which only the style and the three stigmas are dried and used. It adds a very distinctive rich golden-yellow tint to this dish, but its flavour is really quite mild.

We travelled by boat, obviously, as that's the only way to experience the spectacular coastline from Vilanculos to Bazaruto Island, which is located at the tip of the Bazaruto Archipelago. As our feet hit dry sand we were welcomed with smiles, tropical flower necklaces and island-style cocktails - and this was just the beginning. This speck in the ocean definitely gets my vote for a perfect island getaway. It's exquisite for snorkelling and diving and, most importantly in my book, boasts some of the best game fishing in the world. This was one opportunity that I was not going to pass up.

As a consequence 'Cooked' changed to 'Hooked' for this episode. But once again all the talk of easy fishings jinxed my chances and, first up, the only thing I managed to lure was a little Boney, which is inedible.

I was pumped, though, that at least it was caught on camera, which was obviously a sign that my luck was changing. The next day was make or break for me, so out to sea we went. This time the fish gods, maybe even Neptune himself, were on my side and I landed a Bone Fish, also on camera for all the world to witness, nogal! This has got to go down as one of the top five places we visited and for fishing it ranks Number One.

SUSHI

'COOKED'-STYLE

Creating sushi is just as much a craft as it is a culinary experience. While in Japan they believe that it takes as much as ten years to become proficient in this art form, if you follow my two simple rules you'll love what you produce. Truth is, if I were a purist I'd call mine sashimi not sushi - it's just one small portion in the sushi spectrum and it will take a little longer for you to master the entire palette. However, this is my creative contribution on how to serve beautiful fresh firm fish that's as pleasing to the eye as it is to the palate.

There're only a couple of rules when it comes to my brand of sushi. **The first**, and by far the most important, is that the fish you use is so fresh that it's still flapping. **The second** is that you use a razor-sharp knife to slice it ultra thin - about 3 mm slices of raw fish fillets - then arrange nicely and serve as is.

If you like, offer a good low-sodium soya sauce, wasabi (hot green Japanese horseradish) and gari (pickled ginger) as accompaniments - not that fish this fresh needs any flavour enhancers.

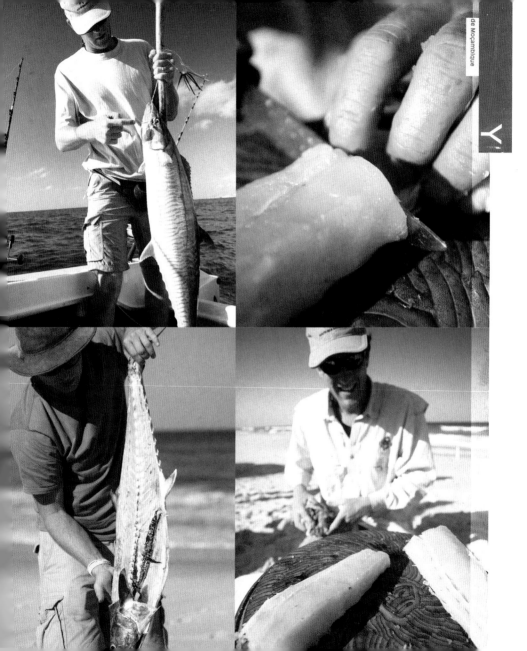

We were lucky enough to make this on a tropical beach in Mozambique, but it's equally lekker when made for mates on the braai in my back garden. We used kuta, or king mackerel, but any oily fish (like yellow tail) will do just as well.

CASHEW NUT BARBECUED KING MACKEREL

YOU NEED

1 x 500 g deboned fillet of king mackerel with the skin left on

2 handfuls of cashew nuts

100 ml olive oil

piri piri sauce
(blood hot chilli sauce)

4 ultra ripe tomatoes

2 stale bruschetta
(or pão if you're in Mozambique)

8 cloves of garlic - *peeled*

handful of salad leaves including peppery rocket

1 lemon cut into wedges

sea salt to taste

Make a paste by crushing the cashew nuts with a drizzle of olive oil and a splash of piri piri sauce - think of the consistency of peanut butter. Rub the whole fish fillet with olive oil and place skin side down on a cutting board. Use your hands to smear the paste all over the flesh side. Chuck the tomatoes on the braai to roast and sweeten. Place the whole fillet, skin side down on a grid and cook until the skin goes crisp and brown. As this was a hefty piece of fish, and was as thick as it was long, it was cooked for a further two to three minutes to ensure it was cooked right through. Cut the bruschetta in half and toast on the fire until really crispy, then rub the garlic cloves and pap tomatoes into the toasty bread so that they can be absorbed.

Lay down a layer of salad leaves on the bruschetta, place sliced rounds of the fish on top and add more leaves, drizzle with lemon juice and olive oil and eat immediately.

The basic principle is that when wood burns, the smoke from the fire seals the meat and adds radical flavour. This process of preservation has been around for ever. When man discovered fire, he accidentally discovered smoke as well. I just like the flavour the smoke imparts and if you thought it was too complicated and way too much effort, think again.

SMOKING FISH

THE DIFFERENCE BETWEEN HOT AND COLD SMOKING – *Hot smoking* is quicker and takes anything from a matter of minutes to several hours. It's used for fish, meat or chicken and involves placing the food directly above the fire, or in an enclosure that is heated directly by the fire. The temperatures reached in hot smoking will kill any microbes in the food. *Cold smoking* takes many hours, sometimes days, as the smoke passes by the food that is placed in an area separate from the fire. Generally the food remains at room temperatures during the smoking and no cooking takes place. So the inside texture of the food isn't affected and nor are any microbes present in the meat or fish. For this reason cold smoking has traditionally been combined with salt curing, particularly in foods like cheeses, bacon and cold-smoked fish like trout.

Firstly, hot smoking fish requires an oily or fatty fish, normally game fish - think snoek, think tuna, think shad, think harder or mullet. In my opinion, this is better because oily, fattier fish seem to stand up to the smoke, which adds lovely flavour. So head off to your fishmonger and ask him to scale and butterfly your choice. Very importantly, the skin must be left on as most of the flavour *(collagen)* in fish is in the skeleton and skin. So lose the skin to your own gastronomic detriment. Next up, you have to dry the fish. There are two ways to do this. The first is quicker and easier but ultimately affects the flavour. Pat the fish dry with paper towel or, better, salt the fish with a couple of handfuls of salt - I like to use coarse Maldon sea salt - and let it rest for 20-30 minutes *(depending on the size of the fish)*. Then rinse off all the salt under running water and dry the fish well using paper towel. Hang in a nice cool windy spot until the fish is tacky to the touch *(about 2-3 hours)*. Now the fillets are ready to smoke *(Follow the method given on page 110)*.

TO SERVE Take your fish out of the smoker. Place a couple of knobs of butter on the fish. Eat immediately with fresh bread, a green salad and a glass of your favourite white wine. If there are leftovers, or you overdo the fish *(and there is a good chance that you might)*, they can quickly be made into pâté and eaten on Melba toast within two days. This is a great alternative.

SMOKED FISH PÂTÉ

250 g oily fish - *I used Kuta*
¼ cup cream
**small knob of butter
  at room temperature**
juice of 1 lemon
salt and pepper to taste

Smoke your fish, and then let it cool. Remove bones and skin.
Flake the fish and combine with the rest of the ingredients using a fork. You could use a blender, but doing this by hand means you get a chunkier pâté. Season and serve with fresh bread or crackers.

We had aimed to be on the water at 7am sharp and to spend the morning leisurely paddling to the Isle of Pigs where we would be treated to a local-style lunch. But as a result of a colossal jol that had played out the night before, our group only staggered out of bed somewhere closer to 10. Finally we were on our way - our intended destination a rustic little island restaurant that specialised in local food. Set up as a community initiative, visitors kayak to the island and are treated to a slice of the true Mozambique experience, and in return the locals can earn much-needed income.

What's not often evident when watching our show is the lengths to which we go - in this instance, paddling like crazy in an attempt to catch up with the schedule. By the time we arrived the babbalas had really kicked in and all I could think of was a beer to quench my thirst. But we were blown away by the massive welcome we received from the island's children and before we could say 'beer please' there was a soccer match on the go, using a home-made plastic ball. It escalated quickly, attracting both friends and crew. The pitch had no boundaries and roughly spanned the length of the island but the enthusiasm was infectious and headaches were quickly forgotten. Without a doubt the kids were the highlight of our visit.

I remember thinking at the time that lunch was a fairly humble affair of ripe tomato salad, freshly baked bread, rice and lovely local steamed crab. Am I kidding! You won't find fresh crab of this calibre on the menu of the hottest seafood restaurants in any major SA city. The lunch wasn't gourmet, but who wants that anyway? It was simply superb.

This is a little something that we prepared at **Justino and Garth's Casa** - our little makeshift open-air eatery on a deserted Mozambique beach in the middle of nowhere.

MOZAMBICAN CEVICHE

Ceviche is a method of preparing thinly sliced fish by 'cooking' it - not by conventional heat but rather by allowing the acidity in lemon juice to denature the proteins. This keeps it firm and brings out the fantastic sea flavour.

In this case we used freshly caught Kuta that we cut across the grain into about 3mm thick slices. Then we laid the fish on finely chopped onion and covered it in fresh lemon/ lime juice, a sprinkling of sea salt and a good splash of coconut water. Just for a little extra kick we chucked in a dash of the potent local devil *(chilli)* sauce. Make sure the liquid just covers the fish then place in the fridge for about 20 minutes and it's ready to chow.

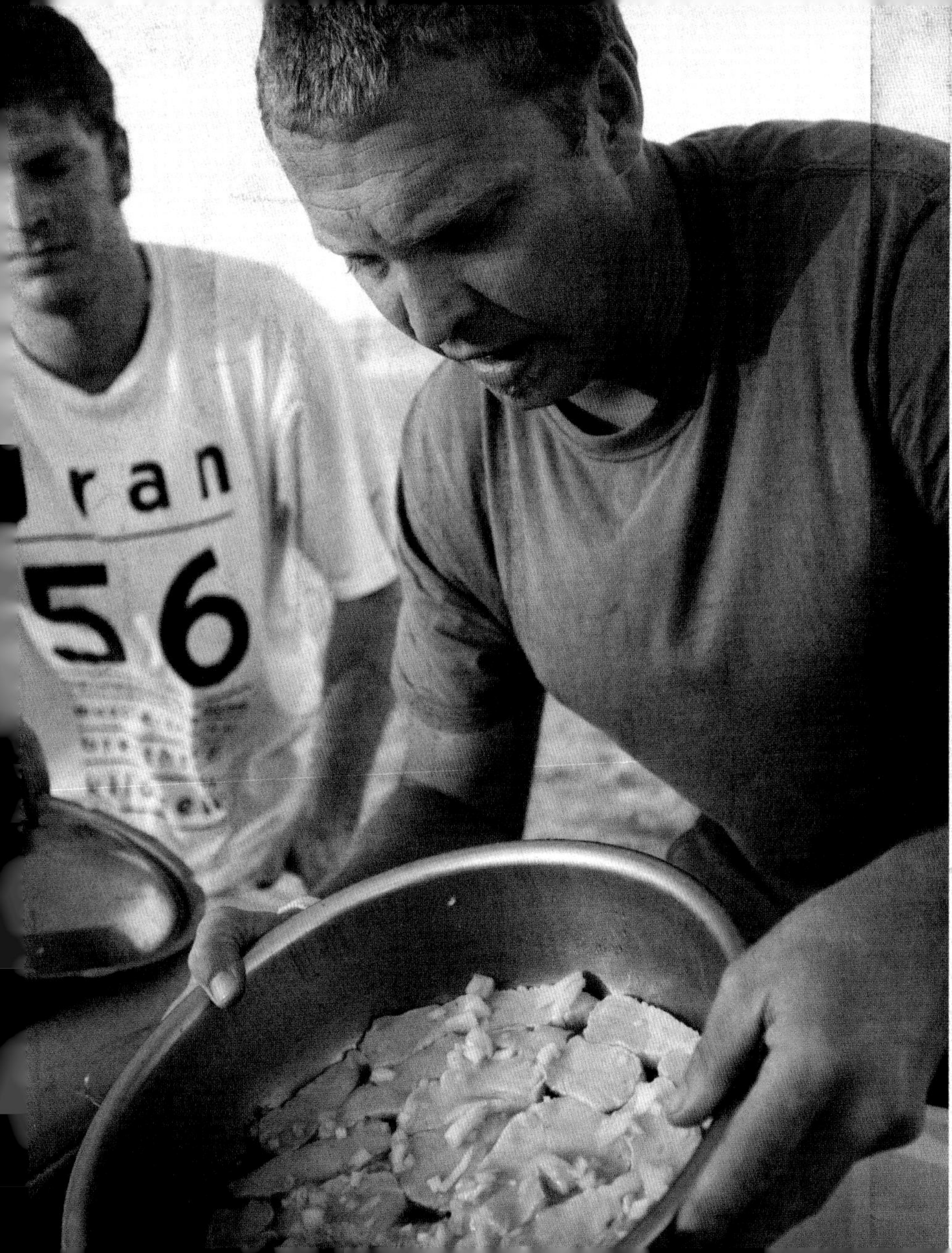
ran
56

As a committed locavore who is convinced that this is the greener option, I try wherever I am to eat foods that are locally fished, farmed, grown or produced. Let's start appreciating and taking care of our weird and wonderful creepy-crawlies of the deep, and making a point of finding out where our food comes from. Fortunately for us, Mozambique hasn't entirely sold out to the international market and when we were there we were able to pick up some beautiful top grade local produce.

GIANT LULA STEAKS WITH A SUN RIPENED TOMATO & CALAMARI SALAD

★★★★ THIS RECIPE SERVES ABOUT 20 ★★★★

Cut the calamari tubes into steaks and score them horizontally at 1 cm intervals. Before frying, blanch them in boiling water for a count of exactly 20 - not one second longer. Dump them in cold water immediately to cool and then pat dry. This will help to make them melt-in-the-mouth tender.

Meanwhile, slice the small cherry tomatoes and a few large sun ripe ones as well. These are the two varieties that are sold everywhere in Mozambique, so that's why I used them. But you should pick up whatever is going at the local organic market. Add the onion, garlic, coriander leaves and spring onions.

When you're ready to eat, pan fry the calamari steaks in a mixture of olive oil and butter for extra flavour. The trick with calamari is to cook it quickly - so just one minute per side and they're ready.

When cooked, take a couple of the steaks and cut them into strips and drop them into your 5-star tomato salad. Finish off with a mixture of local honey and a little fish sauce. Toss one last time and then serve with the rest of the steaks.

YOU'LL NEED

about 1 kg fresh whole calamari

a handful of small cherry tomatoes

a few large sun ripe tomatoes

1 onion - *sliced*

fresh garlic - *chopped*

fresh coriander leaves

a handful of spring onions

olive oil

butter

honey

fish sauce

I chose to film the last episode of the second season of Cooked on the historically significant beach of Robben Island. In recent times this has become the best-known 550-odd hectares of real estate in the Cape, but this wasn't always the case. What is not so well known is that way back in the day Autshumato, the strandloper chief who was fondly referred to as 'King Harry' by passing sailors, was banished to the island on two occasions for misdemeanours against the newly arrived Dutch settlers. This was more than 300 years before Nelson Mandela met the same fate at the hands of the apartheid government. As they say in the classics, the more things change the more they stay the same. And this also applies to this simple two-ingredient dish that was probably part of Harry's staple diet and tastes just as brilliant today. So if you and your partner ever land up on a desert island, try it.

STRANDLOPER CRAYFISH

For two people

YOU'LL NEED

2 fresh crayfish
a drizzle of seawater

Make a fire with hardwood. I go for apple wood if it is around, because the wood of fruit trees imparts great flavour when burnt, but use whatever is available. Clean the crayfish by placing them belly side down and cutting from the tail to the head. Remove the thin dark entrails and rinse the crayfish in fresh seawater.

When the flames have died down, place the crayfish shell-side down directly on the coals. Cook until the flesh of the crayfish changes from translucent to white and the shell turns red - about 5 minutes. Then turn them over and cook for further 3 to 4 minutes.

To serve, pull the perfectly cooked flesh out of the shell, drizzle with seawater and eat immediately with your bare hands - just like Harry would have done.

Can you imagine anything more idyllic than spending a spring weekend with 19 mates lazing on a houseboat moored on the tranquil lagoon at Langebaan on the West Coast? Langebaan is one of a series of quaint historic villages which include Lambert's Bay, Paternoster and Saldanha Bay. In case you've never been there, it's about an hour's drive from Cape Town.

SNOEK

Around these parts snoek *(a member of the snake mackerel family)*, mussels and crayfish are staple food, and in August and September the surrounding fields are carpeted with flowering wild daisies, succulents and other brightly coloured fynbos.

(1) **Stuffed Butternuts, Potatoes and Sweet Potatoes on the Braai** Wash all the veggies well and pat dry. Halve and de-pip the bulb of the butternuts, then fill the cavities with blanched and chopped spinach, feta, butter and parsley. Rub oil and salt on the outside of the potatoes then wrap all the veggies in tin foil and braai on the coals, turning the potatoes regularly for an all over tan. You'll know the butternuts are cooked when the sides squash in easily and the potatoes when a sharp knife slides through them with ease.

(2) **Strawberry Dressing for a Green Salad** Place halved strawberries in a bowl. Add 2 tablespoons sugar, balsamic vinegar and chillies to taste. Mix and allow to stand so that the juice from the berries is drawn out and forms a thick syrup which goes beautifully with the snoek. Serve over an array of salad greens, especially peppery rocket.

(3) **Snoek on the Braai** Cut the snoek open along the backbone, from the tail to the head. Remove entrails and head and rinse. Next, cut one incision down the centre of each fillet *(be careful not to cut through the skin)*. This increases the surface area of the fish, and what you are left with are two butterflied halves. Down in the Cape this vigorous form of gutting and butterflying a snoek is called 'vlekking'. Whack with salt and allow to stand for 20 minutes. Rinse and pat dry.

Melt a large knob of butter in a saucepan, then add a handful of roughly chopped chillies *(seeds & all)*, a couple of chopped garlic cloves and apricot jam to taste. Combine all ingredients thoroughly. Liberally rub the sweet and sticky marinade/ glaze well into the flesh side of fish - be careful because the bones are prickly! It's best to do this once it's on the braai. Place flesh side down on medium heat - that is, when you can hold your hand over the coals for about 8 seconds before it gets too hot. Watch the butter and jam turn golden brown. Then turn fish over to skin side but don't leave too long - allow for about 4 - 5 minutes per side. *Get stuck in, but watch out for those bones.*

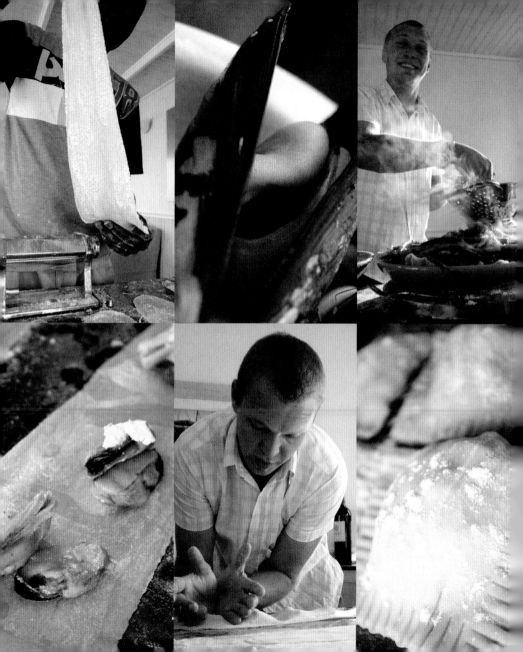

RAVIOLI STUFFED WITH MUSSELS

20 fresh black mussels

a glass of dry white wine

a large bunch of fresh parsley

a large knob of butter

fresh pasta...

2 cups flour

2 eggs *(free range or organic)*

★ ★ ★ ★ **THIS RECIPE SERVES 4** ★ ★ ★ ★

① **STEAMED MUSSELS FOR THE FILLING -** Drop the mussels into a pot and break a handful of parsley over them. Pour over the wine and stir well, replace the lid and steam over a medium heat for a few minutes. Take a peek now and then. As soon as the mussels open remove the pot from the heat. Discard any that haven't opened, as they were probably dead when you picked them. Retain the juice at the bottom of the pot. It's full of flavour, so strain it and add it to your tomato sauce a little at a time.

② **HOMEMADE TOMATO SAUCE** (next page)

③ **FRESH PASTA -** Place the flour on a clean flat surface and make a well in the middle. Break the eggs into the centre of the well and, using your *(clean)* fingers, gently mix the egg into the flour. Once the egg has been absorbed knead the dough for about 10 minutes - pretend it's play dough and have some fun, just don't drop it on the floor! Wrap it in cling wrap and refrigerate for about 20 minutes. If you want a richer dough, use just the yolks from 3 eggs, instead of the 2 whole eggs.

④ **FAT IS FLAVOUR -** In the meanwhile cut off a decent stuk of room temperature butter - mix it thoroughly in a bowl with a couple of finely chopped cloves of garlic and some parsley. For those of you who, like me, are partial to the tingle of fire on their tongues, make a second bowl with the same ingredients, but this time add a few chopped chillies.

⑤ **MAKE THE RAVIOLI -** Sprinkle some flour on your work surface to prevent the dough from sticking. Using your hands, make balls about the size of golf balls; put them through the pasta machine on its thickest setting through to its thinnest, until you have the desired thickness. This will give you a long, flat, broad piece of raw pasta, roughly 3 mm thick. Cut this into squares - 3 fingers x 3 fingers. Place small spoonfuls of flavoured butter and a steamed mussel in the centre of each. Fold into triangles: using your finger, start from the corner and gently push the edge down easing out any air in the pockets. Pinch the edges with a fork to make sure that the ravioli don't explode into a soggy watery mess when you cook them. Repeat until all the filling has been used up.

Drop the ravioli gently into a pot of salty boiling water. Cook until al dente - this'll only take a couple of minutes so keep your eye on these guys. Drain, plate and smother with your rich tomato sauce. Serve with generous shavings of Parmesan and lashings of good olive oil.

If all you've ever done in your life is boil water, it would be a good idea to learn to make this simple sauce before you learn anything else. It'll stand you in good stead with many recipes in this book - and, in fact, throughout your future culinary life.

HOMEMADE TOMATO SAUCE

In a pan, fry the garlic and onion in the olive oil and butter until the onions are clear and have softened. Add the fresh and canned tomatoes. Break up the anchovies with your fingers and add them. Lastly add the strained juice from the steamed mussels in the previous recipe, a little at a time, tasting before adding more. Let this all simmer, not boil, for about half an hour until the fresh tomatoes have disintegrated into the sauce. If you prefer a thicker sauce, allow to simmer with the lid off for 10 minutes or so before serving.

Ouma's Trick: If the sauce is too acidic for you, add a pinch or two of sugar to make it mellow out.

You'll need

2 cloves of garlic
- *peeled and roughly chopped*

1 peeled white onion
- *thinly sliced*

3-4 tablespoons olive oil

knob of butter

4 vine-ripened plum tomatoes - *roughly chopped, skin and all*

1 tin whole peeled tomatoes

2 anchovy fillets

When you decide to break away for a few days, leave your troubles behind but keep your conscience with you; it won't take up any extra space. So don't fill up with groceries and fresh produce before you go, source as much as possible once you get to the other end. Most of what you need for these hearty recipes can be picked up at local farmers' markets and best of all they'll be free range and organic. Otherwise ask around for a good butcher, a local independent brewer or winemaker, an enthusiastic market gardener and poultry or dairy farmer - these guys will be only too happy to sell you some of their home grown produce. Small town folk are moerse friendly and generous and they'll probably fill your boot with all kinds of lekka goodies, and wouldn't it be great for the kids to be able to see where their food actually comes from so that they can feel a sense of connection to their dinner for a change.

LOCAVORES
03
ARE LEKKER PEOPLE

There's something very wrong about not knowing if what's in your pot at least lived a contented, healthy and reasonably fulfilled (although somewhat shortened) domestic life. So while you may be thinking that by saying 'free-range' I'm just jumping on the ever-popular hybrid bandwagon, in all honesty I'd rather know that my food was reared humanely than be munching away at mountains of cheap meat just because I can.

FREE RANGE CHICKEN AND CHUTNEY POTJIE

★★★★★ **THIS RECIPE SERVES 4** ★★★★★

My mom got this recipe from an old man many years ago and it's always been a real winner with my family and anyone else who's tried it. When I was growing up it was served with barley or brown rice, but it's equally good with pap or creamy mashed potatoes. You decide.

Light a fire and once the flames have died down place your potjie directly on top of the coals. Toss a good splash of oil in the pot and allow it to heat up. Put the chicken pieces in the pot and let them caramelise all over. Keep your eye on the prize and make sure they don't burn. Remove the chicken and set aside. Fry the onions in the remaining oil until they begin to brown.

Throw the potatoes and chicken into the pot. Add a bottle of spicy chutney, a cup of cream, a handful of dried apricots and salt and pepper to taste. Give the pot a good stir and put the lid on. Now shift the bulk of the coals aside, leaving just a few under the pot - the cast iron will retain the heat well. Keep a separate fire going on the other side of the braai and add coals when the ones under the potjie are no longer producing a sizzle - roughly every 20 minutes. Simmer gently for about an hour, or until the meat is just about falling off the bone.

What you'll need

cooking oil

8 pieces of chicken
 - *I like to use thighs but you can use whatever pieces you like*

2 onions - *chopped*

4 medium potatoes
 - *parboiled and cut into slices*

a bottle of home-made spicy chutney

a cup of cream

a handful of dried apricots

salt and pepper to taste

I don't know what it is about wide open spaces but I just love the great outdoors. I'll visit isolated areas anywhere, anytime, anyhow. One of these is the Fish River Canyon in southern Namibia. It's truly one of the natural wonders of Africa and it gives you such a high when you look down over the edge where the earth drops half a kilometre below the Huib Plateau. This boldly beautiful chasm just bellowed for us to explore its rare bare essence.

On the day before we cruised down into the canyon proper, we stopped over on the southwestern edge. From here we could look out at the flat-topped mesas and the 1500-million-year-old exposed rock and earthy colours. Our camp was pitched on the vast plain where zebra and buck, including springbok, have for centuries grazed on the sparse grasslands. In the distance the only links between the earth and the sky were the erect quiver trees, named by the San who used their hollow branches as quivers. It seems as if there's always been an eternal contest between man and beast - our forefathers used arrows, snares and, finally, rifles to hunt for the pot. I wanted to honour the tradition - only difference being that I sourced my meat from a butcher in the area, and the local red wine is a lot better than any of the brews concocted by our ancestors.

I chose springbok neck, which has very little fat and, like all tougher cuts of venison, is best cooked very slowly in a three-legged potjie. Since the Dutch introduced this widely used pot to Africa over 200 years ago it's been used for everything from stews to brews and is also great for breads. Because of this is it affectionately known as the Maluti Mountain microwave. I have a collection of potjies of various sizes and never leave home without at least two on a hot standby.

It was dusk by the time the meal was ready and we relaxed with plenty of good red wine. As the sun set and the canyon burst into flames of scarlet and orange, the silhouettes of the massive aloes stood like sentries guarding our camp. In spite of the vastness of the terrain I felt safe and secure enveloped in the arms of the painted landscape.

There's something a little macabre about cooking the national emblem - our dainty Springbok. This little antelope can run at 80 kilometres an hour and leaps in the air for the pure joy of it. But once you've savoured its distinctive flavour you'll appreciate that this elegant creature has more to offer than speed and agility.

SPRINGBOK NECK POTJIE

WITH DUMPLINGS & A DOUGHBOY

★★★★★ THIS RECIPE SERVES ABOUT 6 ★★★★★

If you can't find springbok or get your head around eating venison, you can substitute with neck of lamb. And if you don't have a potjie you can use any heavy pot with a good tight-fitting lid on a tripod. *(But you really should get at least one potjie.)* If you can't cook on an open fire, you can do this at low heat on a hob, but it isn't nearly as energy efficient and unfortunately the whole experience won't be quite as good.

Ideally potjiekos is cooked in the great outdoors over an open fire, but in winter I use mine inside, next to my fireplace. Potjie pots aren't fussy and you can even burn charcoal. Once the cast iron is well heated it needs just the occasional smoldering log or hot coal under its round belly to keep it sizzling happily and very soon you'll begin to recognise its distinctive whisper - reassurance that comfort food is on the way.

You'll need

- about 1½ kg springbok neck - *cut into pieces*
- enough cake flour to coat the meat
- a good dollop of olive oil
- 1 onion - *roughly chopped*
- 3 cloves of garlic - *squashed and chopped*
- 2 teaspoons salt
- freshly ground black pepper - *to taste*
- a sprig of fresh rosemary
- 1 cup good red wine - *sun-kissed warm*
- 1 cup meat stock - *warmed*
- 2 leeks cut into thin rounds
- 2 carrots cut into rounds - *they add a lovely light sweetness*
- ½ butternut cut into chunks - *I leave the skin on as it helps the pieces to stay whole*

Coat the meat in flour and brown in hot oil in the potjie pot to seal. Remove the meat and set aside. Add the onion and garlic and sauté until the onion is translucent. Reduce the temperature of the pot and add the meat, salt, black pepper, rosemary, wine and stock and give it a good stir, then put on the lid and leave to simmer on gentle heat for 2½ to 3 hours until the meat is tender. It is very important that the dish just simmers *(the potjie pot whisper)*. If the meat boils rapidly it will become tough and taste like old leather so, please, no rushing . . . gentle heat only. When the meat is starting to become tender layer the leeks, carrots and butternut on top of it, without stirring. Replace the lid and cook for a further 20 minutes. Now add the doughboy and the dumplings.

FOR DUMPLINGS AND THE DOUGHBOY

2 teaspoons baking powder
500 g cake flour
big pinch of salt
grated pecorino cheese
large knob of butter
about 1 cup of cold water

Sift the baking powder, salt and flour together. Add the pecorino cheese, and then gently rub in the butter with your clean fingertips. Gradually add cold water until you have a soft dough. To make the doughboy, roll out a piece of dough and cut out or model a gingerbread man and place it on top of the veggies at least half submerged in the gravy in the centre of the pot. Break off small pieces from the rest of the dough *(about half the size of a chicken's egg)* and place around the doughboy. Put the lid on and cook for a further 20 minutes.

Important! // No peeking or the dumplings will flop.

Now dish up, sit back and enjoy with a glass or two of good red wine.
Take good care of your potjie pot and it'll be around for years. After using, wash it thoroughly in hot soapy water and when it's dry rub the inside thoroughly with a little vegetable oil – this will prevent it from rusting.

No. 74

6632 2015

2.7

KOLMANSKOP

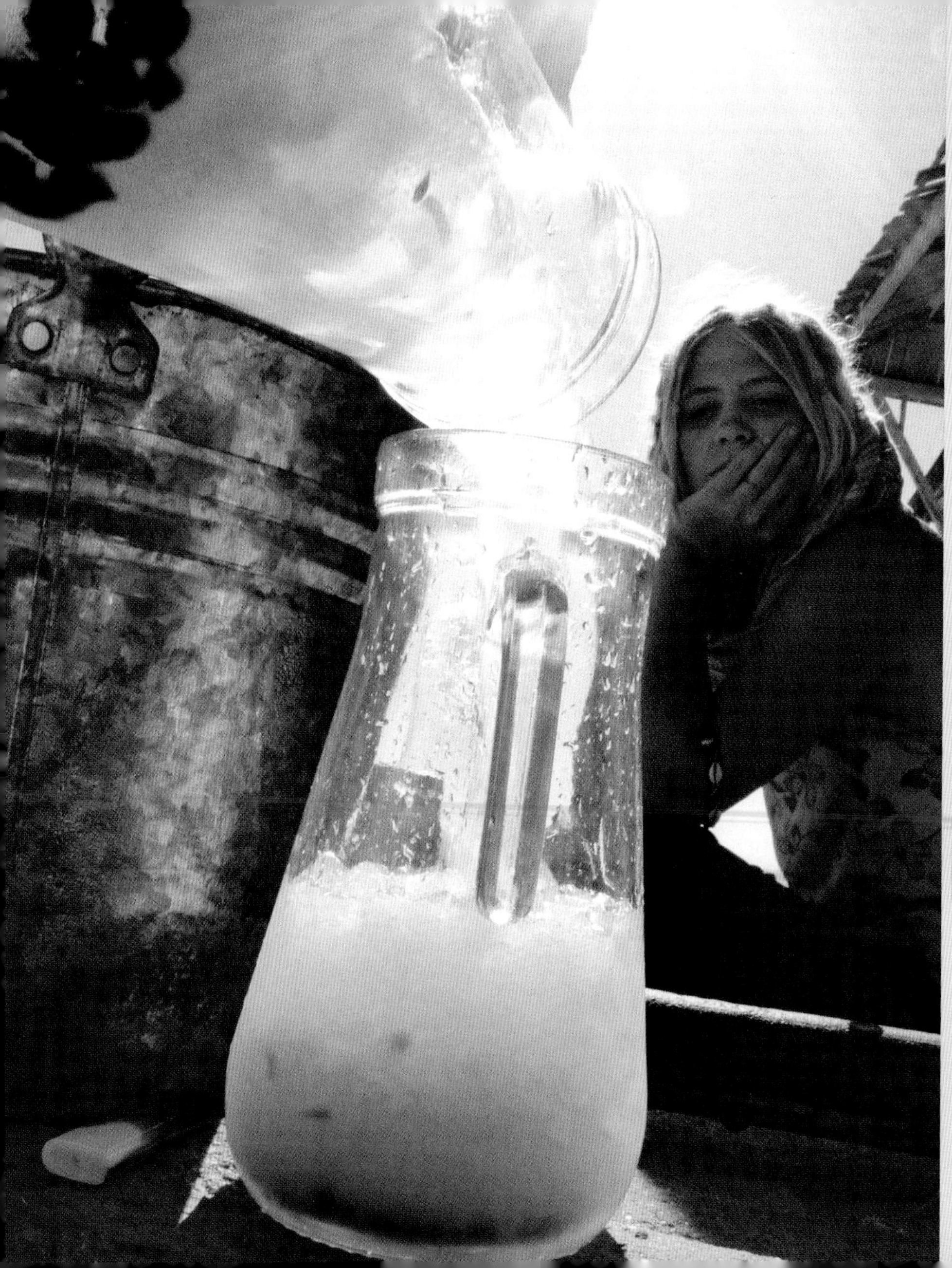

Quite a little gem in its time, this derelict diamond-mining town has turned into a dry gulch. Sadly, even the ice factory no longer operates and we could have done with a ready supply on the day . . .

HOME-MADE LEMONADE

If you ever need something to lift your spirits and wet your whistle, try home-made lemonade. We certainly needed some when we hit the hot and dusty ghost town of Kolmanskuppe and this effervescent drink just hit the spot.

THE TRICK IS TO REMEMBER THE RATIO: 1 cup sugar: 1 cup water: 1 cup of lemon juice (which is roughly 5 lemons). If you prefer it to be less sweet, cut down on the sugar a little.

 MAKES ABOUT 6 GLASSES

INGREDIENTS

1 cup sugar - *reduce to ¾ cup if you'd prefer it less sweet*

1 cup water

1 cup lemon juice

a handful of raisins

cold water and ice - *so that you can dilute to taste*

The secret to perfect lemonade is to make a simple syrup by dissolving the sugar in warm water so that it's dispersed evenly instead of sinking to the bottom. So if you have a stove handy, heat the sugar and water in a small saucepan and stir until it's completely dissolved; otherwise just stir very well. Extract the juice from the lemons. I use my Grannie's juicer but you can do this anyway you like. Pour the juice and sugar water into a jug, throw in the raisins and leave for a while, overnight if possible, to allow them to start fermenting and give it a fizz. Before serving add about 2 cups of cold water and a bag of ice to the jug - more or less, depending on how strong you want it to be. If the lemonade is still a little sweet for anyone's taste, chuck a slice or two of lemon into the glass.

SOUSSOSVLEI 2,8

SPICY CHICKEN LIVERS

This is another little recipe where simplicity is truly key. Fry chopped onion and a couple of heads of garlic in a splash of olive oil, then add chicken livers. In the mean while make a fresh chilli relish with the following ingredients: **chillies (I like little potent buggers, but if you prefer larger sweeter ones go ahead and be boring!), coriander leaves, lemon juice, extra virgin olive oil and sea salt to taste.** Mung the ingredients together in your trusty pestle and mortar.

Once the chicken livers are cooked allow them to chill and then chop until they have a fine textured consistency. Now combine the chilli relish and the chopped livers and mix together thoroughly in a small shallow bowl. Pour melted butter over the top to preserve. Serve whenever, with toasted rounds of pão.

Note that I haven't given exact quantities here, as I find the best versions of the recipe are achieved when guided by personal taste preferences rather than instruction.

PS: You can add a splash of cream to give it a smooth rich texture but, hey, that's up to you.

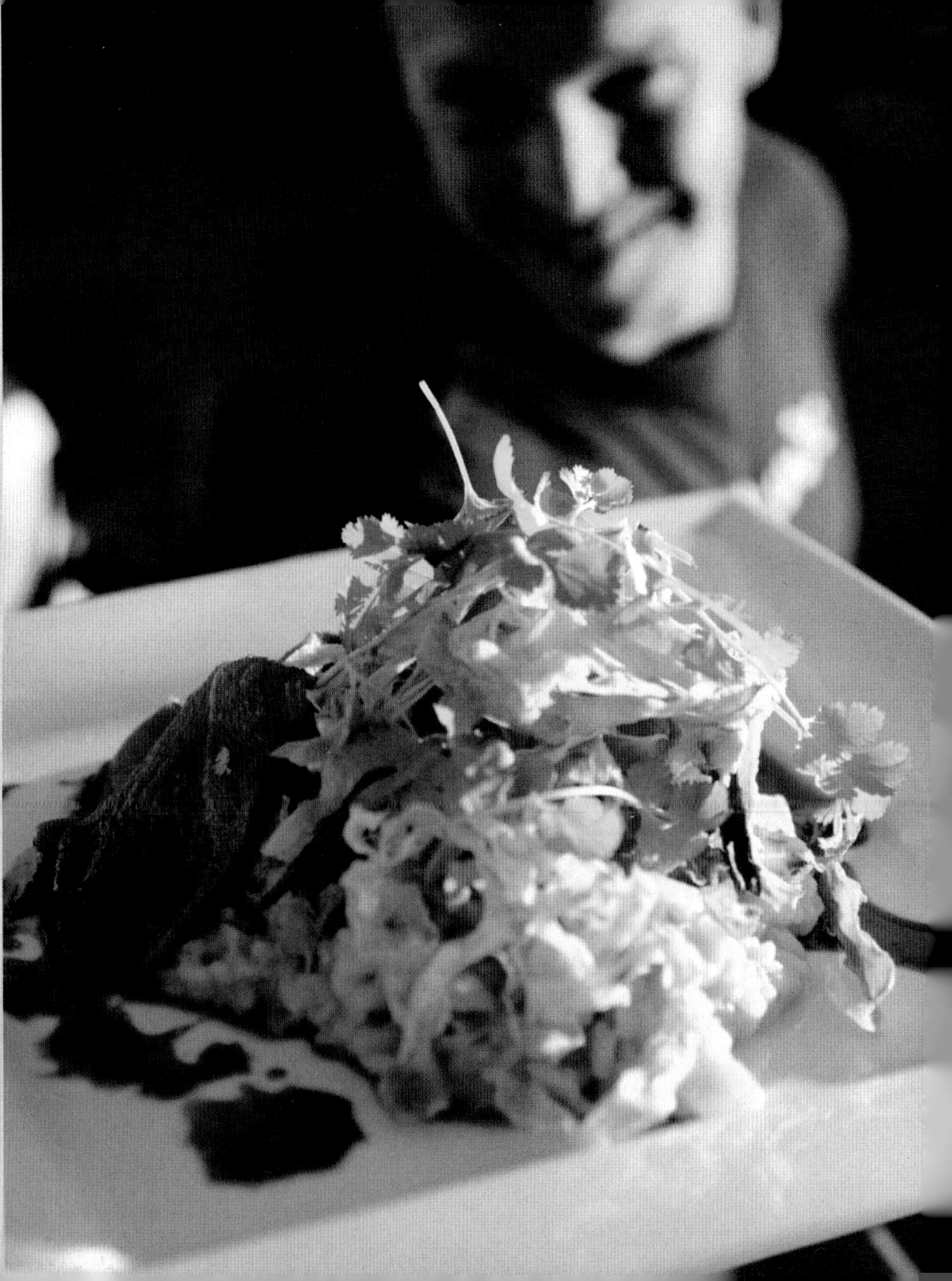

BUTTERNUT AND SWEET POTATO RISOTTO

✶ ✶ ✶ ✶ ✶ **THIS RECIPE SERVES 6 - 8** ✶ ✶ ✶ ✶ ✶

This is one of the very few times when I would say that too many cooks improve the broth, so ask a mate or two for help.

Melt the butter in a pan over a low heat. Add a splash of olive oil to prevent the butter from burning. Add the onion and allow to sweat until translucent. Add the garlic and fry for 30 seconds. Add the risotto rice and stir until the grains are coated with the butter/olive oil. Add more butter if you like - this dish can never be too rich. Turn up the heat and add a ladle of stock. When it dries up, add some wine, stirring continuously. When the wine has been absorbed, add more stock, and continue this process of alternating between the wine and stock, and stirring continuously, until the rice is cooked. The rice should be al dente and creamy, with every grain separate. Season with salt and pepper to taste.

After you've added the third or so cup of stock, ask for some assistance with shaving pieces of butternut and sweet potato into the pot. The only way to know for sure when the risotto is ready is by tasting, so try a little. It should take roughly 30 minutes to cook.

Serve with a side dish of sweet potato and butternut crisps and a few slivers of ostrich carpaccio.

Carpaccio *was first served in Harry's Bar in Venice in the 1950s. It's named after a Renaissance painter who used a lot of red in his art, because originally it consisted of wafer thin slices of mature raw beef which had been drizzled with a cold vinaigrette made from olive oil and lemon juice. Nowadays very thin slices of almost any tender cut of raw red meat and even firmer fish like tuna which is 'cured' in this way is called carpaccio.*

INGREDIENTS

a big knob of butter

a splash of olive oil

1 onion - *chopped*

4 cloves of garlic
   - *peeled and chopped*

2 cups Arborio (risotto) rice

1 litre vegetable stock

1 cup white wine

salt and pepper to taste

1 small butternut - *peeled*

1 medium sweet potato
   - *peeled*

a handful of butternut and sweet potato crisps

a few slices of ostrich carpaccio

This recipe will open your eyes to the value of home cooking and life will never be quite the same again. You'll chuck out the tinned spaghetti and meatballs - strands of soggy gluten and heavy sawdust balls floating in tartrazine-preserved tomato gruel which, as a last resort, you force down after a blinding night out when you can't see your way clear to turn on the stove. Now just the thought of a bowl of fresh pasta and home-made sauce will have you feeling molto bene!

FRESH SPAGHETTI
AND BAKED MEATBALL SAUCE

INGREDIENTS FOR SAUCE

a couple of cloves of garlic
- *peeled and roughly chopped*

some onion
- *peeled and thinly sliced*

a good dollop of olive oil

a knob of butter

about 3 vine-ripened plum tomatoes
- *roughly chopped, skin and all*

a tin of whole peeled tomatoes

a couple of anchovy fillets

First prepare the fresh pasta *(see next page)* - or, at a push, you can walk pasta the dry stuff and get some fresh from your Italian deli . . .

Then make the sauce - and, while you're at it, you might as well peel and chop enough garlic and onion for both the sauce and the meatballs.

① TOMATO SAUCE

Method // In a saucepan, fry the garlic and onion in the olive oil and butter until the onions are translucent. Add the fresh and canned tomatoes. Break up the anchovies with your fingers and add to the sauce. Cook for about half an hour on low heat *(it must simmer, not boil)* until the fresh tomatoes have disintegrated into the sauce.

What you should know about anchovies: *They taste nothing like anchovy paste. Even if you try one and think it's a little strong on its own, once they've blended in they become that secret ingredient that gives the sauce its zing. A jar is quite pricey but lasts a long time, and once you're converted you'll find plenty of ways of using them.*

② MEATBALLS

While the sauce is simmering, turn on your oven to 180°C and bake the meatballs. This is a healthier option than frying in oil as the fat in the meat will bake out and can be discarded before the meatballs are added to the sauce. We all need to watch our cholesterol!

Method // Chuck all the ingredients into a bowl and mix thoroughly with clean hands. Roll into 3 cm balls, arrange on a baking tray and bake in the preheated oven for 10 minutes. Don't overcook – you want to end up with juicy, plump taste-bombs, not hard cannon balls. They'll cook through when you add them to the tomato sauce.

Meanwhile, give your sauce a stir and a taste. You might want to add another anchovy fillet. Just a suggestion!

. . . .

Fresh Pasta Rules - you're tongue-dead if you can't tell the difference, capiche!

. . . .

Method // Place the flour on a flat clean surface and make a well in the centre (think volcano). Break the egg into the well and mix gently with clean fingers. When the egg has been absorbed, knead the dough for about 10 minutes. If it's too dry, add a splash of water; if it's too wet, sprinkle more flour. It should have a rich golden colour and the texture of play dough. Wrap it in cling wrap and refrigerate for about 20 minutes.

Sprinkle flour on your work surface so that the dough does not stick to it and, again using your hands, make a small ball out of the dough. Flatten it out with a rolling pin or wine bottle. Keep rolling until the pasta is as thin as possible because when it cooks it doubles in thickness. Cut into thin strips, about ½ cm wide, and hang over the back of a chair to dry.

Five minutes before eating . . . drop all the meatballs into the tomato sauce, stir and heat through. Cook the pasta in rapidly boiling water for about 3 minutes and then drain. Watch it like a hawk because it gets soggier much more quickly than the dry stuff.

. . . .

To serve // Dish up the pasta and smother with tomato sauce and meatballs. Add freshly grated Parmesan cheese and a twist or two of black pepper. Serve with a green salad on the side.

INGREDIENTS FOR MEATBALLS

500 g lean beef mince

2 cloves garlic
- *finely chopped*

1 onion - *finely chopped*

a handful of basil leaves
- *chopped*

a handful of grated Parmesan

salt to taste

freshly ground black pepper to taste

INGREDIENTS FOR PASTA

1 egg - *free-range and organic*

1 cup of cake flour

Invest in a pasta-making machine. Hand rolling takes time and extra effort, and once you know the value of fresh pasta you'll want to invest in a hand-operated machine. They are not very expensive and most brands are good – just make sure that you're able to vary the thickness so that you can make all sorts of pasta, from spaghetti to lasagne.

ROOIBOS SMOKED TROUT RAVIOLI
WITH BURNT GARLIC AND TEQUILA SAUCE

'Country people are the ones who invite you into their hearts and homes and who blow you away with their kindness and generosity. Ja, the country people . . .'

They're great . . . and so is this recipe, the one that I made while my mates relaxed alongside a beautiful farm dam in the Hogsback district. Only fly in the ointment that day was my lack of luck with my fly in the water. Here, surrounded by mountains, forests, waterfalls and dams bursting with trout I felt a million miles from anywhere and it was easy to understand how this place was such an inspiration for J J R Tolkien's fictional Mirkwood Forest in The Lord of the Rings.

I'm not sure if it was the ancient Afro-montane trees or the overwhelming sense of stillness but I, too, felt the urge to produce, not a best-seller, but lunch for everyone. So at the crack of dawn I set out to bag me a trout. Our host's dam was the perfect setting and I felt confident, but the pressure of having promised to provide the key ingredient for our meal finally got to me and I think the trout must have sensed my anxiety. It never ceases to amaze me how these little devils, with a brain the size of a pea and a memory span of three seconds flat, manage to outsmart really skilled fishermen. But the locals lived up to their reputation for generosity, and one who'd been luckier *(or smarter)* than me was kind enough to sense my humiliation and come to my rescue.

So after building up an appetite on a gentle hike - not up the mountain, just through the forests to the waterfall - we settled down next to the dam to prepare my much-vaunted trout ravioli.

After the humbling experience with the rod I needed some Dutch courage. Thank goodness the recipe calls for a bottle of Agave Gold Tequila and a shot glass. I recommend that you klap a shot before starting - it certainly got me going!

For smoking the fish, you will need . . .

a smoking dish - *the bottom half of an ordinary deep roasting pan will do just fine*

tin foil - *enough to line the pan and cover to seal*

a fish grid or flat wire grid that fits into dish

. . . as well as . . .

1 deboned side of a medium-sized trout

4 rooibos teabags - *tea leaves removed from the bags*

1 tablespoon of honey

pinch or two of Maldon sea salt

For the filling . . .

Flake the smoked trout into a dish, add a fist-size piece of ricotta cheese and mash roughly.

For the sauce . . .

2 large knobs of butter

a head of garlic
   - peeled and sliced roughly

6 large tablespoons honey

1 tablespoon cayenne pepper

1 tablespoon paprika

3 shot glasses tequila

½ litre cream

matches - *preferably long ones*

1 good pinch of salt

For the ravioli

2 cups flour

2 eggs *(free-range or organic)*

SMOKING   Sprinkle rooibos leaves evenly over the bottom of the smoker or the foil-lined baking pan *(shiny side up)*. Sprinkle salt and drizzle honey all over the fish. Place skin side down on smoking grid or wire/fish grid placed in pan. Close up or seal the baking pan with foil *(shiny side down)*. Place over hot coals for between 7 and 13 minutes, depending on the thickness of the fish. Remove from the heat.

TIP: If you don't want to use rooibos tea, you can use any hardwood sawdust - think oak or apple wood, but not resinous wood *(like pine, bluegum etc.)*. Most fishing shops and good supermarkets stock decent sawdust, and one bag will last absolutely ages as you only use about 2 tablespoons at a time.

THE SAUCE   Offer everyone a shot of tequila then reward yourself for getting this far. Melt the butter in a non-stick heavy-based pan, add garlic and fry until crispy, but not burnt. Add honey, cayenne pepper and paprika and stir gently while increasing the heat to max. Then leaning away from pan, add tequila and light it using a long match. Burn off all alcohol *(the huge flame will eventually disappear)*. Remove from the heat. Add the cream, put back on the stove and heat while stirring until the sauce is hot, but not boiling *(otherwise the cream will separate)*.

MAKING THE RAVIOLI   Place the flour on a clean flat surface and make a well in the middle. Break the eggs into the centre and using clean fingers, gently mix the egg into the flour. Once the egg has been absorbed knead the dough for about 10 minutes. Wrap it in cling wrap and refrigerate for about 20 minutes.

Sprinkle some flour on your work surface to prevent the dough from sticking. Using your hands, make small balls and put through the pasta machine on its thickest setting. This will give you a long, flat, broad piece of raw pasta, roughly 2 mm thick. Cut these lengths into squares - 3 fingers x 3 fingers. Place small mounds of trout and riccota mixture in centre. Fold into triangles. Starting from the corner, and using your fingers, gently push pasta edges down easing out any air pockets. Pinch the edges with a fork to make sure that the ravioli doesn't explode into a soggy watery mess when you cook them, and put to one side.

COOK THE RAVIOLI   Bring a pot of water to boil, add salt and then gently drop ravioli into the boiling water. Cook until al dente *(roughly 3 to 5 minutes)*. Drain and put straight into the pan of sauce.

Serve immediately. This is the only time that it's acceptable to spear your trout - as they float gently in the sauce.

4

HOT TOYS

FOR THE MANNE

L adies, when you get the chance to break with domesticity for a few days you want to forget all about cooking and cleaning and keeping the other half and the kids happy, not so? Now, if you play your cards right and bet the boys that they are incapable of building a spit braai or preparing a Tarzan roast, they will get stuck in and have the kids fetching and carrying for them, and you'll have all the time in the world to sit back, put your feet up and kuier. It works every time. We just can't resist a challenge or the opportunity to do a little showing off.

More time to enjoy my Rolex . . . My plastic lighter, pinched by James and my heirloom Rolex, originally my dad's, have more in common than you would think. This has nothing to do with their cost and everything to do with their value. No matter how careful one is, during their lifetime they'll pass from one owner to the next: the Rolex because no one is able to hold on to life long enough, and the lighter because no one is able to hold on to it long enough.

3½ weeks

18 days

1 day

20 hours

243 days

How much I smoke matters to the Rolex because this affects how soon it'll be passed on and how much I smoke matters to the lighter because this affects how soon it'll pass out. I look at it like this . . . I get happy when the lighter moves on or passes out because this means I'll live longer and have more time to enjoy the Rolex before I pass out and it moves on. Wow, look at the time . . . you'll have to excuse me while I pop down to the café to replace another 'lost' lighter.

46 seconds

7 days

43 days

57 minutes

6 days

DRUNKEN BIRDS FOR THE BOYS

When we decided to go on a boys' only fishing weekend in Dutoitskloof the lads said it sounded a little tame so I came up with just the thing to liven things up - a couple of steamy birds.

This is a super simple recipe that combines two of man's favourite pastimes - braaiing and cracking a can. Add 2 juicy chicks and how can it go wrong? Chuck the garlic, pepper and salt into your pestle and mortar and mung the flavours together. Now add a good splash of olive oil and parsley - just bruise the leaves. Use this marinade to give the birds a good old massage all over, inside and out.

When the coals are ready, crack open the beers, take a swig of each and perch the well-oiled birds upright on the open cans, wriggle them down so that they're comfortable and the cavity is filled - we don't want them falling over. Then settle them on the grid and close the Weber. Allow the chickens to cook for between 40 to 80 minutes. The secret here is that the beer boils and steams the flesh from the inside giving it that malty flavour and keeping it juicy while the Weber acts like a braai/oven and crisps the skin.

Who needs other birds when these are so plump and tender!

First off - get the heat up and light a fire in your Weber.

THEN TAKE:

2 whole chickens
2 cans of ale
4 cloves of garlic
whole black pepper corns
Maldon sea salt
olive oil
a small sprig of flat
  leafed parsley

1•1

TOMATO BRUSCHETTA WITH BRANDY FLAMBÉED

SPADE STEAK

This has to be done on a fire for obvious reasons. Take a spade *(not a shovel)* and clean it well to remove all sand and grit and then put it directly on the coals to sterilise. When it's piping hot - you'll know because the shaft will be hot to the touch - rub the fillets in olive oil, then pat thoroughly with the steak rub and place them on the spade. They're going to sizzle - that's the whole idea. Let them cook for about 2 minutes per side - ostrich fillet should be served rare.

Now comes the interesting part. Flambé the steaks by splashing a generous amount of tipple over them. It's going to flare up so stand back and be careful. When the brandy's burnt off, remove the fillets and let them rest for a few minutes so that all the juices are absorbed into the meat before you carve. If you are feeling particularly carnivorous, cut into medallions and chow as is, without the bruschetta and greens.

In the mean time cut the bruschettas in half and toast them on the fire until they're really crispy but not burned. If you don't have a grid, you can toast them on the spade. Once toasted, rub the raw garlic clove over them. This will add a fresh and fiery flavour to this gourmet open sandwich. Roast the tomatoes on the grid or spade until they're pap, then cut them in half and rub them into the toast so that the juices and flesh of the tomato is absorbed into the bread. Then cover with a layer of salad leaves and onion slices. Place the sliced medallions on top of this, drizzle with olive oil and eat immediately.

YOU WILL NEED

2 ostrich fillets

olive oil

1 bottle of brandy

2 stale bruschetta

4 ultra ripe whole tomatoes

4 cloves of garlic

a handful of salad leaves, including peppery rocket

1 onion - *sliced*

1 clean spade

THE BEST STEAK RUB

1 teaspoon of:
- coarse sea salt
- brown sugar
- dried garlic flakes
- mustard and coriander seeds
- white, black and green peppercorns
- paprika
- bell peppers
- 1 or 2 juniper berries

Toss all the ingredients into a pestle and mortar and get bashing - what you are looking for is a fine granular rub to coat the hunk of meat.

Nothing shouts Special Event louder than lamb on the spit. When the occasion arises and you want to go big, get a whole lamb and cook it Greek Style. Choose your day well in advance, invite the mates, stock your fridge with beer and retsina, and be prepared to dance the hasapiko.*

GREEK STYLE LAMB
ON THE SPIT

SCORING THE LAMB // It's important to find a good butcher who understands meat. He needs to make sure it's well hung and trimmed. Give him your numbers - my guess is about half a kilo per person. If you don't have a fridge big enough to keep the lamb cool until you're ready to cook, chuck it in the bath and cover it with ice. Your honey may get a little sour about this, but the rewards will be sweet when she tastes your meat.

HOW TO BUILD A SPIT BRAAI // This spit was designed and thrown together by my friend and me in 10 minutes, so just follow my lead.

① Drill 3 holes 5 cm apart starting 5 cm from the top of the 4 cm diameter uprights, big enough to fit your butcher hooks.

② Dig a pit about 20 cm deep and 50 cm x 180 cm wide and long.

③ Using a mallet *(or a big piece of wood)*, hammer the 4 cm diameter steel uprights into the ground on either side of the pit until only half the upright is sticking out. Remember that the holes must face the length of the pit and be on the same side.

④ Insert butcher hooks into the drilled holes. These holes are used to adjust the height of the lamb above the fire - up is cooler, down is hotter.

YOU'LL NEED

- 2 x uprights of hollow square steel
  - *4 cm diameter, 100 cm long*
- 1 x spit pole of hollow square steel
  - *2 cm diameter, 200 cm long*
- 7 x crosspieces of solid round steel
  - *0.5 cm diameter, 20 cm long*
- 2 x butcher hooks *(or bend your own from pieces of steel)*
- small roll of galvanised wire
  - *1.25 mm gauge*

HOW TO ATTACH THE LAMB ① Push spit pole through the lamb's back passage until it is centred on the pole. ② Secure 2 x crosspieces in front of chest and behind back legs with galvanised wire. ③ Secure 2 legs together (intertwined) at the end of the shanks with galvanised wire. Repeat for both front and rear legs. ④ Poke wire through the back of the lamb to secure the spine to the spit pole in 4 or 5 places from the neck to the pelvis and twist tight with a pair of pliers. Once attached, check and remove any missed fat without damaging the meat.

HERB RUB

a handful of fresh/dried oregano leaves

a handful of rock salt

a handful of crushed garlic

juice of about 5 lemons

BASTING SAUCE

1 litre lemon juice

a handful of fresh/dried oregano leaves

a handful of coarse salt

a couple of cloves of garlic - *crushed*

Oregano. This herb is an integral part of Greek cuisine and gives the flavour to the lemon and olive oil that accompanies so many of their fish or meat grills and casseroles. It's easy enough to grow and always good in stews and sauces – stick some in a pot if space is available.

The **hasapiko is an ancient Greek butcher's dance. Maybe you could invite your friendly local meat man and teach it to him – might mean a discount on your next order and he'll certainly be invaluable when it comes to the carving!*

PREPPING THE LAMB

① In the pit make a fire using 2 bags of charcoal - never briquettes. Centre the fire under the chest and hindquarters - these are the thickest parts of the lamb and the heat radiated from here will cook the waist and ribs. To check if the fire's hot enough, hold your hand about 30-40 cm above it - if you can keep it there for a count of 5, good. Remember to keep the heat up by adding more charcoal every now and then right through the cooking process.

② Combine all the ingredients for the rub in a bowl and mix well. Wash the lamb thoroughly with water. I use a hosepipe and give it a complete blast to make sure it's clean. While it's still wet, rub the paste all over and leave to dry and get down to ambient temperature.

③ Place the lamb on the spit 30-40 cm above the fire and start turning. What you're looking for is about 14-15 turns a minute on a motor-driven spit or once every minute if turning by hand. This is going to take at least 3 hours, so get your mates to help turn and reward them with cold beverage that'll keep them happy but don't overdo - you all need to stay focused. The first hour or so heats the meat up to cooking temperature and then the real cooking starts. If there's a little wind or the day's overcast, it may take longer. During the first hour or so any fat on the lamb will drip into the fire and flare up, so keep a bucket of water handy to kill any flames.

④ At the 1½-2 hour mark make the basting sauce. Combine all the ingredients in a bowl and mix thoroughly and then baste every 5 minutes or so. At about the 2½ hour mark the shoulder blade will start to pull out. This is a sure sign that the meat is getting there. Give it another ½ hour and it should be ready. You can also check by inserting a sharp knife into the thickest part of the hindquarters – if the liquid runs clear, the lamb is cooked. If the liquid runs red, it's not done yet, and if it's pink then the lamb is rare and needs just a little longer. When there's 10 minutes or so to go, brush with beer for that lovely malty taste.

CARVING Once it's ready to carve, move the coals to one side and place a tray under the lamb. Carving a whole lamb can be a little intimidating. The trick is to take it in sections. Start by cutting away the hind legs. The meat should be very tender and come apart pretty easily. Work down through the shoulders and separate out the forearm sections. It helps if there are two people carving, but in any case take your time and you'll get there. Invite honoured guests and future family members to help themselves, because this is one killer meal that should be eaten hot.

The red-sand sea of the Namib is the most diverse desert on earth and Klein Aus Vista offers wild horses, diamonds and dunes - strong medicine that called for a powerful antidote, and I had just the remedy.

SPIKED
WATERMELON

If you're squeamish around needles or can't handle hard tack then this operation might not be what the doctor ordered. On the other hand, this potion works wonders for people who don't shy away from the cut and thrust and need a little more than a medicine measure of melon-flavoured balm to raise their spirits.

All it takes is a watermelon, a bottle of vodka and the largest syringe, with needle, that you can find.

The trick is to inject as much vodka as possible into the flesh of the watermelon - don't be afraid, this baby can handle a healthy dose. Jab it all over and if any vodka starts to seep out patch it up with a plaster. Now cool this tonic down, either in the fridge or in a cooler box full of ice - the colder it gets the quicker it'll take effect. When you're feeling up for it, slice off the peel, dig in and heal yourself. Gesondheid!

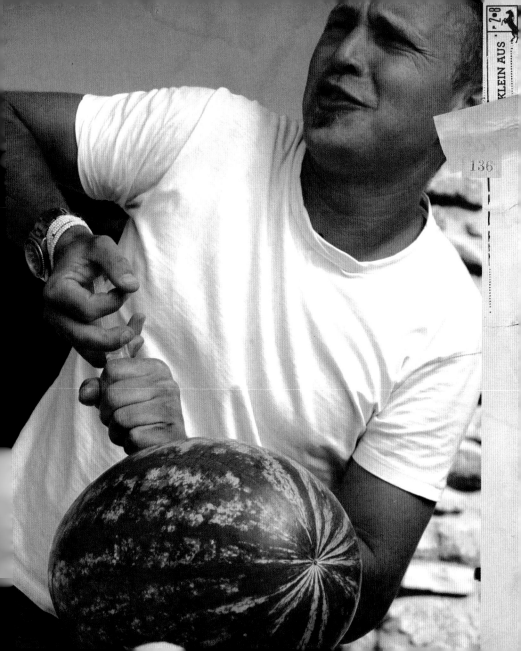

136

MARSHMALLOW TREE // The Acacia erioloba or, as it
is more commonly known, the CAMEL THORN TREE grows
ear-shaped pods that are to heffalumps what honey is
to Winnie-the-Pooh and as a consequence they'll pretty
much go to any lengths to get their trunks on them.

We followed their lead - just added our own sweetmeat.

In the upper reaches of the majestic Olifants River Valley this hideaway on stilts in the middle of a poplar forest brought out the primeval male in me and I was tempted to swing from the branches and yell . . . FIRE! About two million years ago, somewhere along the southern tip of Africa, man discovered quite by chance that ripping off large hunks of meat and chucking them in the flames did startling things to the flavour. From that day forward the heat's been on and no dassie or duiker, eland or elephant or any other four-legged herbivore, wild or domestic, has escaped a roasting. We've developed a myriad of hot variations and every red-blooded male has an arsenal of braai techniques. I, too, have a few strings to my bow but once in a while I'm forced to admit that another guy's idea is a killer. This one goes to Braam Kruger in whose amazing book Provocative Cuisine I first discovered this primordial method - he calls it Tarzan Roast . . . and, by Jane, it rocks! You may recognise it by its ancient name - a Poacher's Roast.

TARZAN ROAST

COOKING METHOD

✴ ✴ ✴ ✴ ✴ **THIS RECIPE SERVES 10 - 12** ✴ ✴ ✴ ✴ ✴

Lay the leg of lamb on its side in the baking tray and, using a small sharp knife, cut slits 3-5 cm deep at a 45 degree angle all over the lamb. Force rosemary sprigs, chilli and garlic slivers into the slits, then dip the spring onions in the oyster sauce and force them in as well - the green leaves will jut out, a bit like a porcupine! Mix together the oregano, the balance of the oyster sauce, the onions and the juice from the lemons and orange, and pour this all over the leg of lamb. Leave to marinate while you make the fire in the wheelbarrow.

The meat actually cooks by radiated heat and is gently smoked at the same time. I usually use orange or apple wood because of their aromatic properties and I make the fire in a wheelbarrow. This is useful because the cooking time is somewhere between 4 and 6 hours, and during that period of time Mother Nature could blow hot and cold and change her tune a number of times. But with a wheelbarrow you can adjust the position of the fire and take full advantage of the prevailing wind.

READY TO COOK First, slip the wire through the shank and twist it so there's no chance of the meat falling into the fire. Attach the wire to the rope with a slipknot.

• •

THE TREE Once the leg is attached to the wire and the rope you need to find a nice strong branch in a tall tree from which to hang your meat. *(Be sure that it's far enough away from your house and any dry tinder. You don't want to end up chasing a runaway fire.)* Again using a slipknot attach the rope to the branch and then, between the wire and the tree, make a sheepshank knot in the rope - this way, you can adjust the height of the lamb as required. Balance the baking tray with the left over marinade on a stool and position this directly under the joint. Wheel the fire in next to the stool and place it so that the prevailing wind is blowing towards the lamb. You should be able to hold your hand between the fire and meat for just a few seconds without burning it. If it's not hot enough chuck a couple of extra logs on the fire to really get the heat going. You can use the forked stick to push the leg closer or further from the heat. And that's it. For the next 4 to 6 hours, you need to keep basting the lamb with marinade and the fatty juices that drip into the tray. Every 10 to 15 minutes turn the meat about 45 degrees and secure its position with the forked stick.

• •

VERY IMPORTANT: Keep testing the heat and adding a log when necessary. Otherwise, your early evening meal could turn into a midnight feast.

Slip Knot

Sheepshank Knot (ironic)

about a 3 ½ kg fatty leg of lamb, with the shank intact - *very important*

a few sprigs of rosemary

a couple of whole chillies - *as hot as you can handle*

10-15 cloves of garlic - *peeled and cut in half*

3-4 bunches of spring onions

¼ cup oyster sauce

a handful of dried oregano

2 onions - *sliced*

the juice of 2 to 3 lemons

the juice of 1 orange

. . . as well as . . .

a baking tray

about half a metre of galvanised wire

2-3 metres of rope

a forked stick

a basting brush

a sharp knife

a small stool

a wheelbarrow - *useful for both braaiing and gardening*

orange wood - *any hard fruit wood will do, but do not use ordinary firewood*

an accessible branch on a tree that is not too close to your house

While you're rolling the joint and smoking it . . .

We were fortunate enough to make our manly meal in the Cederberg where there was plenty of space to let off steam, but if you're not lucky enough to be able to get out into the great outdoors don't despair, take a stab at it wherever you may be. Just remember this macho way of cooking a hefty hunk of lamb takes mega time and if you hit the jungle juice and form a laager with a lager too early things could get really hairy. One way of avoiding this is to take some time out to get in touch with your sensitive side. Include the ladies and absorb the bits of nature that suburbia has on offer. First up, turn on your sprinkler *(it's good for cooling off any coals that sneak out of the braai)*, but just long enough to get the lawn damp enough to bring out the earthworms which will attract the birds. Then take off those boots - being kaalvoet so that the mud can squelch between your toes is essential. Now get down and do some sky gazing. Encourage your mates to join you as this is an excellent time to get your lawn weeded. I'm not prescribing total abstinence - basking while sipping slowly from Bohemian glass goblets *(or cracking a can, if you must)* gets the mind juices flowing and leads to some beautiful banter. Be on the lookout for birdcalls, butterflies and bugs. Just don't forget to turn your meat! After 4 hours or so of chilling, poke a skewer into the thickest section of the joint to see if it's cooked. If the juices ooze out red, it's still raw and needs more cooking; pink juices mean the meat is perfectly medium rare. When it is cooked, raise the leg or remove the heat and let it rest for ten minutes.

SERVING SUGGESTIONS

I normally carve the meat while it is still hanging up - that way, if it's a bit too rare closer to the bone, you can just drop the roast back near the heat and cook it for a bit longer. So, finally, you've got this pile of perfectly smoked lamb and a group of ravenous mates. Now what?

Option ① - Hands On Grab pita bread. Slice open to make a pocket. Stuff with shredded lettuce, roughly chopped tomato, fresh basil, medium rare lamb and a good dollop of Greek yoghurt. *Don't wait . . . get stuck in!*

Option ② - Serve with Root Veggies Start preparing at about the 3-hour mark. Chop all the veggies into pieces about the same size so that they will all be ready at the same time. *Use: baby potatoes, beetroot, parsnips, carrots, sprigs of rosemary, olive oil.* Preheat the oven to 180°C. Blanch the various vegetable types separately in boiling salted water for 10 minutes. Place on a baking tray, add the rosemary and drizzle with olive oil. Slow roast for between 40 minutes and 1 hour, turning occasionally. Once they're cooked, reduce the heat of the oven to its lowest setting to keep them warm. While the roast is resting make a sauce by pouring all the drippings and scraps of lamb in the baking tray into a pan, mix a teaspoon of cornflour in a cup of milk and add this to the pan. Keep stirring on low heat for between 5 to 10 minutes until the sauce begins to thicken. To serve, place vegetables and slivers of roast lamb on a platter and drizzle the sauce over the meat. *No need to stand on ceremony - help yourself!*

For centuries people have used pit ovens for cooking out of doors. It's nothing more than the slow, even release of heat within a sealed hole in the earth and things cooked this way stay juicy and flavoursome. Since no flame or fire ever reaches the food, there's no danger of it burning. You should think of this as an underground slow steam cooker.

BUILDING A PIT OVEN

To get started, you need a whole load of igneous rocks, the kind used in a sauna. Metamorphic and sedimentary rocks contain water and will explode when heated and you'll be pulling shrapnel out of your mates' backsides *(or worse)*.

1. Gather a whole lot of fist-size igneous rocks.
2. Dig a hole approximately three times the size of the food you're going to cook. Keep the soil to use later.
3. Line the bottom and sides of the hole with the smaller rocks.
4. Make a fire in the pit with lots of wood and charcoal.
5. Once the fire is burning well build a pyramid of rocks around it.
6. Let the fire burn down until the rocks collapse - this will take a while.

TIPS If you don't remember your school geography, igneous rocks are formed by the solidification of cooled magma *(molten rock)*. A simple - but not foolproof - test is to bash two rocks together. If they're igneous, they'll generally make a ringing sound.

When cooking bigger animals in your pit oven, it's advisable to cut the meat into a number of smaller pieces so it'll cook faster and more thoroughly. For some reason vegetables take longer than normal, so parboil them before chucking them in the pit oven.

Since the cooking process relies on steam and not dry heat, green plant material is needed to create the steam. For the herb layer you can use any edible leaves except cabbage - these impart their flavour to whatever you're cooking. So be creative!

Estimating the time it takes to cook the food depends on so many variables, but here are some rough guidelines. A chicken takes between 2 and 3 hours, a whole pig will take 6 to 8 hours. Leave for longer rather than less time. If you don't get it right first time, you'll have to finish your meal off on the braai or in the oven, but it's unlikely to come to this.

PIT OVEN CHICKEN

Make a flavoured butter by pulling the rosemary or tarragon leaves from their stems and tossing them into a bowl with the butter, black pepper and sea salt. Use a fork to mash all these ingredients together thoroughly. Slide a finger in between the skin and the meat on top of the chicken breast and create a pocket, then push the flavoured butter into the pocket and massage the bird to make sure the butter is spread evenly under the skin. Drizzle the juice from one lemon all over the chicken. Cut the second lemon in two and pop it into the cavity. The metro-man method is then to dress the chicken in a double layer of tin foil, which works fine but is not nearly as inventive nor as primal as wrapping it in five layers of banana leaves and securing these with a piece of wire or butcher's string. The chicken cooks in its own moisture and the aromas from the green herbs get in everywhere - leaving you with a truly lekker hoender.

For 1 chicken you'll need

a large knob of butter

fresh rosemary or tarragon sprigs - *if you're making two chickens, try one of each*

black pepper and Maldon sea salt to taste

2 lemons

12 washed banana leaves

Rosemary *is that woody perennial with thick needle-like evergreen leaves that give off a strong fragrance when you rub them. It's pretty hardy and easy to grow and if there isn't a bush in your garden you should scout around because there's bound to be one in the neighbourhood. Try to get to know the person who owns it but if that's not possible then it's midnight raid time. Break off a few pieces and plant in full sun at dusk or dawn, water it well immediately and soon you'll be the one guarding your crop.*

TO COOK THE CHICKEN

1. Splash a bit of water on to the stones - they should be so hot that the water evaporates instantly - think of pouring water on to sauna rocks. If they're not hot enough, add more wood.
2. Using a pair of tongs, remove the top layer of rocks. Leave the bottom layer but remove any remaining burning coals.
3. Place three banana leaves on the bottom layer of rocks, followed by a bunch of edible green plants or herbs. More rosemary or tarragon will do nicely.
4. Place the wrapped chicken on top of the herbs.
5. Cover with more herbs and/or the remaining banana leaves, then pile on the hot rocks. Cover these with an old towel or piece of fabric to keep the sand out.
6. Lastly - fill in the hole with the soil and walk away.

It's going to take between 2 and 3 hours for the chicken to cook, but rather err on the side of caution and only take it out after 3 hours. It's impossible to burn your chicken and the longer it cooks, the more likely the meat is to fall off the bone. Just be careful not to get sand in your dinner. This is a primitive method of cooking and so it's only fitting that it's eaten South African style - with your fingers. Try out a small pit oven and do a chicken. When you've built up your confidence go huge and cook a whole lamb or even a pig.

After an incredibly humbling visit to an authentic local home in the Lesotho Mountains, where we were treated to a deliciously simple snack of freshly baked mountain rolls, and I was able to look on and learn how it's done, we hotfooted it down the Sani Pass to the Underberg. Splashy Fen music festival is held on a farm here in the southern Drakensberg every Easter weekend and we were ready to take in the music and cheer on the artists. This event has done a lot to shape authentic South African contemporary music and showcase our very own fusion of styles and cultures. It's been great at fostering a feeling of togetherness between previously diverse artists and, most of all, it's a really good jol. Although it was wet underfoot we stayed high and dry. But before setting off I prepared a little soul food to keep the band and crew rocking for the longest time.

DUSTBIN PIZZA

YOUR OWN PIZZA OVEN IN 15 MINUTES

Before you start, buy yourself a metal dustbin with a lid, or score a 45-gallon metal drum *(the kind that we used to halve and turn into braais)*. These old drums are becoming rare so go down to a scrapyard and have a look around, but first have a squiz because you just might have one gathering dust behind the shed in your own backyard. If you find one, wash it out thoroughly - in fact, give the inside a good scrubbing just to be sure. Also pop down to your local hardware store and pick up two unglazed quarry tiles made from red clay *(terracotta tiles). Make sure they're unglazed or you could end up poisoning the masses.*

If you're doing this at home look for a quiet unused corner in your garden. Lay down the drum on its side and cover with soil. Clay has the best insulation properties of all soil and will keep your pizza oven piping hot, so if this is going to be a permanent fixture *(and, trust me, it will)*, try to get hold of some clay - otherwise use whatever soil you have. Place three bricks on either side of the drum to keep it from rolling and dislodging the soil.

Pastry AND Pizza Roller

Ekco ®

THE BEST PIZZA DOUGH

500 g white bread flour
a big pinch of salt
10 g yeast
325 ml warm water

Combine the flour and the salt in a large mixing bowl. Activate and dissolve the yeast by placing it in a bowl and adding the warm water. *(The water must not be hotter than 45°C as this will kill the yeast.)* Give it a stir, and sprinkle a handful of flour over the mixture to prevent the yeast from forming a crust. Leave the yeast mixture for 10 minutes - it'll begin to froth - and then gradually add it to the flour, mixing it well until it forms a dough. The only way to do this is with your hands. If the dough is too sticky, add a bit more flour; if it's too dry, add a splash more water, and so on. Knead for 10 minutes until the dough has a smooth, elastic consistency. Sprinkle some flour on your work surface, place the dough on the flour and cover with a damp tea towel. Leave the dough to rise for 30 minutes - until it doubles in size. The damp tea towel will prevent it from drying out.

Sprinkle some flour on a clean work surface and then tear off a fist-sized piece of dough. Using your fingers or a rolling pin spread it into a circle about the same size as the clay tile. Make the dough as thin as you like - just be careful not to tear it. The border can be slightly thicker as it will give the pizza a lovely crispy edge when baked. Once you've perfected the base, let your imagination run wild. The numbers of pizza variations you can make really are endless.

READY FOR ACTION

Drain the tin of tomatoes. *(I use the liquid from the tinned tomatoes to make a killer Bloody Mary to sip while I'm doing the rest.)*

Using your hands, mash the tomatoes into small chunks. Season with salt and pepper. Using the back of a spoon, spread the flavoured tomato evenly over the base - not too much or the pizza will become soggy. Drizzle with olive oil, sprinkle over some Parmesan and garlic, rip up a couple of basil leaves, and finally top with pieces of mozzarella and some wafer-thin slices of pancetta.

Make a fire with real wood or charcoal in the back of the drum, never ever use briquettes as they give an awful flavour to anything that you cook with them, and what gives home-made pizza its authentic taste is the wood smoke in the oven. Don't go mad - it's an oven, not a furnace. Next, stack the two tiles horizontally towards the front of the oven and allow them to heat up. The tiles are essential because they ensure that when you bake your pizza, it's heated from the bottom and you end up with a crisp crunchy base. You may need to add another piece of wood every now and then to keep the heat up.

Place your pizza on the heated tiles and tilt the lid over the mouth of the bin to keep it insulated. Crack a cold one, and come back in six or seven minutes, or slightly longer if you prefer a crispier base. Remove and eat immediately.

HOT TIP It's very important always to make sure you have oven gloves on a hot standby. The drum is made from steel, and obviously heats up, so always use gloves when going anywhere near the oven or moving the lid.

If you are too slap gat to make your own oven, at least buy some unglazed terracotta tiles and try this in your normal oven. Preheat to 250°C and bake your pizza for 6-10 minutes. It won't have that lovely wood flavour but it still works pretty well.

MY FAVOURITE PIZZA TOPPING

tin of whole peeled tomatoes
 - preferably Italian

salt and fresh crushed pepper

olive oil - *use any one of the many great local olive oils around*

finely grated Parmesan cheese

roughly chopped garlic *(not the pre-crushed stuff)*

fresh sweet basil

a block of mozzarella cheese - *roughly sliced*

home-made pancetta

SWEETS FOR
MY SWEET

05

Now it's your turn, guys, to regain the upper hand. Well, sort of. I doubt that you'll be able to persuade your better half to do any baking on her weekend away, when all she really wants to do is take it easy, but we men have other things in mind. So knuckle down and measure up and when you present your honey with a deliciously decadent dessert, she's bound to see you in a different light - and who knows what might happen next? She might even agree to let you go fishing with the boys and leave the kids with her.

HOMEMADE ICE CREAM FOR THE KIDS

Rose Petal Ice Cream

(or any other flavour that might add a sparkle to your sweet tooth - think out the tub)

WHAT YOU'LL NEED FOR THE BASICS

1 litre full cream milk
1 litre cream
400g sugar
12 egg yolks

ROSE PETAL SYRUP

4 cups red rose petals
2 cups water
2 cups sugar

① Pour the milk and cream into a large pot and heat gently, stirring every now and then. Meanwhile whisk the sugar and the yolks in a bowl until they become thick and gooey and then add this to the milk and cream. Stir constantly. When the foam has disappeared and the liquid is the consistency of thin custard it's time to add your flavouring.

② The lekker thing about ice cream is that it's a base into which pretty much any flavour can be infused. Once you've added your flavouring, allow the mixture to stand until it reaches room temperature. If it isn't cool before going into the freezer the steam will form ice crystals. Keep your eye on the prize because you don't want it to get rock hard - give it the odd stir. When it's the consistency of soft-serve it's time to whip it out and serve it.

Rose Petal Syrup. Simmer all the ingredients for an hour over a medium heat, and then strain through a fine sieve. If there's any left over bottle and refrigerate, but remember to sterilise the container first.

These sweet treats can be made in two ways. The recipe below is for what we call the boere koeksister, and evidence that the Afrikaners regard this as a national treasure is the two-metre high statue of one erected in their enclave of Orania - unusual, to say the least! Then there is the Cape Malay 'koesuster', which looks and tastes quite different. This is more of a bun that's flavoured with ginger, cinnamon and cardamom, cooked in citrus-flavoured syrup and sprinkled with desiccated coconut. They both have devoted followers and it would be a declaration of war for me to take sides. What I will say is that both are weapons of dietary destruction, so enjoy but know that you'll have to pay the price, or hit the road - take a long brisk walk or, better yet, get jogging!

KOEKSISTERS

INGREDIENTS

For the dough you'll need:

240 g cake flour
4 teaspoons baking powder
½ teaspoon of salt
2 tablespoons of butter
½ cup of sour milk or buttermilk

For the syrup you'll need:

1 kg sugar
2 cups of water
¼ teaspoon cream of tartar
a pinch of salt
grated peel and juice of 1 lemon *(avoid the pith - it has a rather bitter taste)*
1 hand of bruised, peeled ginger

To deep-fry you'll need:

canola oil - which I prefer as it's reasonably priced, good at high heat, and it's the healthier option

★ ★ ★ ★ ★ **THIS MAKES ABOUT ENOUGH** ★ ★ ★ ★ ★

① Sift the dry ingredients together and rub in the butter. Add the sour milk *(or buttermilk)* and mix into a soft dough; knead thoroughly, then leave to stand for about 15 minutes.

② Chuck all the syrup ingredients into a saucepan. Heat and stir until all the sugar is dissolved. Simmer for a few minutes, then remove from the heat and chill *(stick it into freezer for a while to get really cold)*. By now your dough should be perfect for plaiting. Roll out to a thickness of about 5mm and cut into strips 5 mm wide and about 7 cm long. Create plaits with three strips, making sure that you press the strips together firmly at both ends - this is very important because if you don't, the koeksister will fall apart in the oil.

③ Deep fry the koeksisters in hot oil until golden brown - think crunchy outside, but not burnt. Drain quickly and immediately dip into the ice-cold syrup. The trick is to have the koeksisters as hot as possible and the syrup as cold as possible because this way they absorb the syrup better. Once they're saturated remove and leave to set on a wire drying rack.

Take a bite and let the syrup run down your chin. For pure hedonism I like to dip them in freshly whipped cream. But then I'm not counting calories.

Everyone has a story about Long Street where secrets are seldom sacrosanct. Mine emanates from a seedy pub in which I spent many a cold winter evening playing backgammon with mates. When my game needed upping I'd call for another little drop of heaven - a chocolate vodka. For some time the mystery of how to concoct this remained with the barman but my trusty palate and I finally figured it out.

CHOCOLATE VODKA

One massive warning: the combination of alcohol and sugar will rush straight to your brain, so please steer clear of operating any heavy machinery afterwards and of course never get behind the steering wheel . . . And don't let on to anyone how to make it. This is our little secret.

YOU'LL NEED

one third of a bottle of vodka
2 slabs of your favourite plain chocolate

Break the chocolate into pieces small enough to fit down the neck of the bottle and watch them sink into the clear liquid. Put the lid on and immerse the bottle in a pot of warm water for about 10 minutes. As the water heats the vodka it gently melts the chocolate and the two become infused. Put the lid on the bottle and shake until the vodka and chocolate are well and truly mixed. (You may have to return the bottle to the hot water.) What you end up with is a sweet-chocolatey-goodness that's positively lethal. Serve as a shooter or pour over ice cream. If you're really feeling playful, substitute the chocolate with other sweeties - anything from smarties to jelly-babies. But if you are using chocolate keep it straight *i.e. no wafers, nuts or nougat - or it just becomes a soggy mess.*

THANK YOU

The debts of gratitude incurred in the creation of this book are many, but fewer, however, than the number of friends that made it possible in the first place.

My thanks must start with my mom Jeanne, without whom, literally and figuratively, none of this would've been possible. Thanks, Bean.

And then, in no particular order, other than that's how they've popped into my mind, my family and friends: my wife Eugenie, my dad Carlos, my sister Bliss, my son Dan, Richard Mills, Dale Rodkin, Fran Zwiers, Wes Volschenk *(aka Skunky)*, Evan Haussmann *(Eve-Ready)*, Duane Howard, James *(Mom)* Bell, Richard *(Porker)* and Ali Walker, Vik *(Vickie Vale)* Norval, Danny van der Merwe, Bo and Cas van den Zanden, Quint *(Squint)* Bruton, Taz Wilde, Roshni and Erik Haraldsen, Sunel *(Sunella)* Haasbroek, Danny *(Danny K)* Kodesh, Gareth *(Fish Fingers)* and Lisa Beaumont, Eben Smal, Simon Malherbe, Andrew Rawbone-Viljoen, Robbie Fivaz, Jason Abrahamse, Penny Naude, Mireille *(Miggy)* McGregor, Jenny Reay, Gordon Nasser, John Sebastian Esongo, Neil Simpson, Graham *(Brooky)* and Sandy Brookman, Lize and Stewart, Paidric O'Meara, Tamsin Reilly, Nerine Pienaar, Terry Hoffman, John Bull Harrison, Xoliswa Patricia Matana, Garth *(Mort)* Morton, Wilding Penderis, Inka Kendzia, Sean Ou Tim, Melissa Thorne, Darren *(Dad)* Putter, Andy Lupp, Andrew Faber, Evan Maclachlan, Gordon Mcallister, James Warne, Ludgero, Debi Shabason, Kate Kvalsvig, Marlese Lenhoff, Peter Adolphs, Corné Van Rooyen, David Weiland *(who had the faith in my humble idea right at the beginning)* and Keith Floyd *(the first, the one and only)*.

On a serious note: the real rock stars of Penguin who encouraged us to play - more specifically, Louise Grantham, Claire Heckrath, Renée Naudé and Pam Thornley, and to David Schröder, who contacted us with the idea for the book in the first place.

Quint *(funny how one whiskey started our friendship)* and Toby from twoshoes, the best creative team on the planet!

Duane Howard and Evan Haussmann for their mind-blowing photographs.

And last, but not least, Mart Raubenheimer *(Smart)*, my co-writer. Thank you, you rock, brother.

In the words of Ford Fairlane, rock 'n roll detective, you're all un$#&%#@* believable.

Justin
PS: If your name should be here and it's not - OOPS.

INDEX

Once Cooked,
Always Cooked!

Yes Yes,
I know it's
wrong to have
taken the key, but
it's really pretty.

There are some truly moments in my life... Most of them were with Cooked.

Come to the Cooked have we FUNN!!! :)